ANTIQUES ANONYMOUS

Published by Ian Allan Ltd., Shepperton-on-Thames, Middlesex and printed in the United Kingdom by R. J. Acford Ltd., Chichester, Sussex

Antiques Anonymous

A consumer's guide to old furniture

GAY FIRTH

LONDON

IAN ALLAN

Contents

Acknowledgments

THROUGHOUT the preparation of this book I have relied constantly on the researches of experts and connoisseurs whose scholarly publications are indispensable to the student of antiques. I am hesitant to thank by name only a few out of so many, particularly those eminent antiquaries who might not approve of my treatment of their subject. Several are listed in the Further Reading section, but here I most gratefully thank them all, and offer my apologies for any misinterpretation or blunder I may have committed.

I am very grateful to the many friends who tolerated and encouraged me, particularly Mrs Wynne Pierson, who set me on the stony path; Mr Simon Fleet, who taught me much, and Mrs Jack Mackie, whose love and knowledge of antiques are legendary.

Finally I thank Tony Firth, whose criticism was so valid and constructive, and without whom not a single sentence would have been written.

5

Introduction

SOME people collect bank statements; some collect stamps, cats or children. An intimidating number collect antiques, and collecting antiques requires a lot of expert knowledge and a lot of money. You and I don't have a lot of money, and we don't want to collect antiques, and this book is not for people who do.

This book is for those of us who want a chair to sit on or to stand on to reach the picture rail. We eat fruit from a fruit plate: we do not hang it on the wall with a spotlight trained on it; and we do not rope off our dining tables and hang a little sign saying *Do Not Touch*. Most well-made, well-designed, modern furniture is very expensive; and too much medium-priced modern stuff is, by and large, extremely ugly. We know that there is a huge range of objects which fall into the abyss of ignorance called 'antique'; and while we would not actually collect, we could and would use some of them.

Bearing in mind the enormous expense of first-rate antiques, I want to emphasise the merits of 'the Good Second-rate'. For the consumer, as opposed to the collector, this is an important category; it covers the great mass of furniture which is not classy enough to appear in antique exhibitions or in Collectors' Collections: pieces which do not show certain dateable features; little is known about their origin; they may not be genuine period pieces; they simply may not be old enough. These are the Antiques Anonymous, and a lot of them are well worth looking at.

Beware of the really cheap, unless you want junk anyway. The items covered in this book are not junk, and though some may be comparatively cheap beside really good antiques or, for that matter, good contemporary furniture, they still cost money—your money. When it's a question of 'What can I live with that I can afford?' there is a lot to be said for the second-rate antique—with one important reservation: *It isn't beautiful just because it's old*. Your basic knowledge will be valuable only if you combine it with a criterion of usefulness, comfortable shoes and all your willpower.

Oh, you will be lead astray, never doubt it. That rocking chair, that big wardrobe; that card table the man said was Queen Anne— once you get your eye in there'll be no stopping you.

When in doubt, don't. Let that empty space in the hall stay empty: you need it to stand in when you open the door. Sell your mistakes, or give them away, but don't fool yourself that they will be useful—one day. Even the most expensive piece becomes junk if it is cluttering up the house; and non-collectors buy antiques to use, not for their own sake.

6

You will need luck, but not the kind of luck that leads you to find a genuine Chippendale desk lurking at the back of a scruffy shop, with the drawers stuffed with letters from the master to his son, and all for ten guineas—you won't, so get rid of such illusions here and now. Your luck comes with practice, and from a good working knowledge of certain basic styles, designs, and decorative details. A determination not to be taken in and over-charged for a fifth-rate article will be a distinct advantage, too, of course; but the main thing is that you should be able to recognise and criticise what you are looking at. Remember, it's your money.

September 1964.   G.F.

Chapter 1

Scratching the Surface

'ANTIQUE' in a furniture context calls up visions of sales at Sotheby's; shiny new reproductions in the shop up the road; Granny's table mysteriously ruined by the jug of water you placed on it. Designs and dates are for the experts, and Sheraton could be anybody.

Yet, give or take fifty years or so, you know an antique when you see one. It looks old. Not just beaten-up old, but old in a special way: the colour of the wood, perhaps, or the quality of the carving. Maybe the price ticket alone convinces you that a piece is something more than second-hand. As a matter of fact the price ticket can be very helpful when you are sorting out the second-rate from the first-rate and learning what to look for within your price range; but the first hurdle to get over is a clear understanding of what the word 'antique' means.

The non-collector's definition of 'antique' is not nearly so rigorous as the expert's: we are concerned with dates only so far as they help us to identify different styles in furniture. Her Majesty's Customs defines 'antique' as an article proven to be over a hundred years old at the time of buying and exporting; on the other hand, professionals in the antique business lay down strict rules to cover what is antique and what is not. At the present time the year 1830 is the watershed between old and new: this date is arbitrarily fixed and may soon be changed to a later one, but for the time being you will find that no Victoriana appears in the major Antique Fair at Grosvenor House in London.

Non-collectors can afford to ignore both these limitations to the antique market. Our definition is more flexible—and it has to be, for you can be pretty sure that anything actually put together before the beginning of the 19th century is going to price you right into the first-rate category based on age and rarity. High price does not depend on quality alone: it is a safe assumption that the older an article is, the rarer it will be, for the simple and excellent reason that its fellows have worn out—and rarity is what collectors go for. So pre-1800 will probably be beyond us in terms of the genuine article, and we are left with a mere 160 years of cabinet-making to choose from.

Apart from Regency and Victorian furniture styles as such, the 19th century, particularly the last part of it, produced countless reproductions of earlier styles. In our terms, these are antiques. A 19th century copy of an 18th century chair or table is not to be sneezed at: from the consumer point of view it is as good and certainly as useful as the original model, and it will be a fraction of the price. Some of these 19th century copies, of course, will be 'antique' by the narrowest definition; others may not be 'antique' yet, but time is on your side. This is what I mean by second-rate: the problem is how to track these items down.

To recognise the second-rate, you have to know what the first rate looks like. The best way to learn about quality is to study the best examples available: Antique Fairs are held yearly in London and elsewhere about the country, and there is a permanent exhibition of old furniture at the Victoria and Albert Museum. Local museums have smaller collections, and then there are the antique shops themselves, good, bad and indifferent. You should notice which of them are members of the British Antique Dealers' Association: those that are have a blue and gold disc in the window stating the fact. The Association has regulations about honest dealing, and members deal accordingly. This does not imply that non-member dealers are out to swindle you: you are more likely to find second-rate stuff there anyway, but you should watch your step. When you are more or less clear about the major styles in furniture, start asking questions in shops from the smartest to the grubbiest— that chair at 200 guineas: is it a top-quality piece and if so, why? Why is that Regency table more expensive than that other Regency table? Dealers in the high price bracket know their business, and don't be scared to ask. Don't buy it either.

When you see the best, you will understand that top craftsmen spent lavishly in time and materials to produce the first-rate article. There is no skimping: an extravagant amount of wood goes into making a curved leg in one piece; carved decoration is deep and clear; joints are well-finished; the whole thing is properly balanced and structurally sound. Most of the best old furniture was made in London; some of it was specially commissioned, and all of it was relatively expensive even in the good old days—the astronomical prices of today are the combined result of rarity, mystique and snob value.

What we are after in the antique furniture line is furniture in the style of the best, but which is second rate in quality: less ornament less expertly applied; not quite so graceful, not so extravagantly made, but nevertheless in a recognisable style. Taken as a whole, this class of furniture was made by the provincial, country and small-time London cabinet-makers who were less expert and less imaginative than their fashionable colleagues, certainly, but who were nevertheless perfectly competent and very keen to keep up with the current fashion in furniture as the news got around about it. Made on a limited budget for a middle-class clientèle, these second-rate copies and adaptations of high fashion are very adaptable to present-day living; they mix well because they tend to be plain, and while they may be worn and scratched when you see them, the basic structure is sounder and stronger than most of their modern equivalents.

Antiques Anonymous are difficult to date. But then all furniture is difficult to date unless you have inventories and authentic bills of sale from the original workshop. The dates given here are intended only as a general guide to the periods when particular styles were

9

introduced; they peg down a time when such-and-such a design was the height of fashion for furniture belonging to wealthy folk of the day. Don't rely on these dates as you would on an article of faith; and if a dealer assures you with his hand on his heart that the desk in the window is genuine 1783, ask him for proof and don't budge until you get it—and you probably won't, at that. But remember that, unlike today, fashionable styles in furniture and everything else often took several years to percolate down to the out-of-town craftsman. There was no machinery such as television or nationally-circulated magazines to advertise a novelty at speed: a Sheraton design popular in London in 1780 might not appear in Chester until, say, 1790 or even much later. And outside London new styles did not supersede old ones as quickly as they did in the 'beau monde'.

There is a world of honest difference between a price ticket marked 'Chippendale', and one marked 'Chippendale-style'. There is a world of honest difference between a Dior model dress and an off-the-peg copy, too, but at least we know what we are getting—in the antique racket we can never be too sure. The important thing to grasp is Style: second-rate antique furniture reflects the specialities of the master designers and craftsmen to a lesser or greater extent; and as you accumulate knowledge so you will be able to exploit it more and more effectively. So have confidence; and never be afraid to say no.

Chapter 2

Chairs

WHEN a new style in furniture appears, chairs are the first to show it: they are the most sensitive index of furniture fashion. The information given about chairs covers the various period styles in greater detail than the following chapters on other pieces of furniture, so use Chairs as a reference: the dates given will help when you check back to get a fuller picture of a particular fashion. But remember, now and in connection with all early furniture, that fashionable features crop up on reproductions of any date: they do not apply exclusively to period originals.

There is no such thing as The Typical Chair, so make allowances for the fact that there may be lots of divergences from a neat pattern laid down for the sake of clarity. The first lot of features represent a transition from the heavy, elaborate chairs of the late Stuart period to the plain, curvy styles of Queen Anne. If you want to peg them down, you might peg them to the reign of William and Mary.

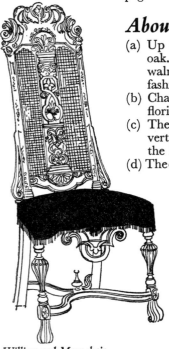

William and Mary chair

* *Refer to Glossary for all words in italics*

About 1690-1710

(a) Up to now furniture had been made of oak. By the turn of the 17th century walnut had superseded oak as the fashionable wood.

(b) Chairs become lighter, and there is less florid decoration.

(c) The lines of the chair back emphasise the vertical, and the back is higher than on the late Stuart chair.

(d) The ornate front *stretcher** and the side stretchers which join the legs on Stuart chairs are now often replaced by a 'tied' *stretcher*: flat or moulded rails running diagonally from the four legs to meet at the centre, where they are topped by a small knob.

(e) Turned (as distinct from square section) legs and back uprights become common. Scrolled legs and stretchers are also used.

(f) The legs often have a square or pear-shaped *capping*, and they may be decorated with fluting or *gadrooning*.

(g) Small shaped *aprons* hang from the seat rails in front.

11

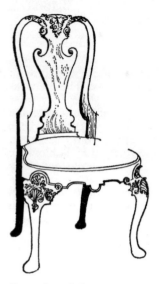

Queen Anne chair

The above characteristics are the shape of things to come; the next group appears soon after 1700, and the points foreshadow the coming Queen Anne style more closely:

(a) The back uprights are narrow and curve slightly to fit the sitter's back; the top rail or *cresting rail* is plainer than the late 17th century example.

(b) The uprights now enclose a solid vase- or fiddle-shaped *splat*, or shaped wooden panel.

(c) The *cabriole leg* appears, often carved on the knee with a *scallop shell motif*.

(d) Stretchers begin to be discarded altogether: the cabriole leg looks best standing free.

(e) The legs end in *club, or pad feet*, and sometimes a *hoof-shaped foot* is used. The *claw-and-ball* foot is not yet common—it becomes very popular from perhaps 1720.

Note that cabriole leg. The curve of this leg is the starting point of a thoroughly curvy era—seat frames, splats, back uprights—hardly a straight line anywhere. Practically every leg is a cabriole for nearly half a century, and during this period a great deal of furniture decoration has something to do with the lion. The claw-and-ball foot and the *lion mask motif* remain popular through George after George after George; the eagle enjoys a smaller vogue, and as ornament changes in the second half of the 18th century we find all manner of flowers, leaves and classical motifs of every kind. For the time being, though, compare this list with the picture of the fully developed Queen Anne chair.

About 1710-1715

(a) The back is now a single hooped line, with no top cresting such as appears on Stuart chairs and, to a less noticeable extent, on William and Mary chairs.

(b) The solid splat down the centre of the back continues into the Queen Anne era.

(c) The seat frame curves; it now has a drop-in seat instead of a cane or an upholstered one.

(d) The cabriole leg is as yet only in front—chairs with four cabriole legs come a little later.

(e) The simple club foot is still in fashion.

(f) The scallop shell is still a popular knee decoration.

So much for early 18th century chair features up to about 1715. On to the Georges.

About 1715-1740

Here we get a change in taste and a change in wood. Mahogany begins gradually to take over from walnut for the best furniture, and plain, simple designs become more elaborate at the hands of Early Georgian stylists. You could call it 'Queen Anne Plus'. The outlines stay basically the same, and these are the extras:

(a) The chair back is lower than the high backs of early 18th century chairs; and the hooped outline changes back to a top cresting rail, whose shape is like a horizontal 'cupid's bow'.

(b) Pierced carving on the central splat comes into vogue.

(c) The knee of the cabriole leg is carved with a lion's or a satyr's mask, or with a *jewel-and-leaf motif.*

Lion mask motif on hipped cabriole leg

(d) The cabriole leg is now often *'hipped'*—in practice this looks like a swollen knee: it curves out as far as the outside of the seat frame.

(e) The *paw, or paw-and-ball foot* is sometimes used with the *lion mask* on the knee (or hip), but the claw-and-ball foot becomes very fashionable indeed. A *scroll foot* is often used on legs with the jewel-and-leaf ornament on the knee.

Mahogany may have been the smart wood for the smart set, but less fashionable craftsmen continued to turn out very fine work in walnut; and it remained popular for ordinary folk like you and me right up to about 1760. Walnut does not last as long as mahogany, and not much Georgian walnut has survived the wear and tear of

more than two centuries of steady sitting; but with a gimlet eye for style and a lot of luck you might stumble on a genuine country-made piece of this period.

About 1740-1800

Within this 60 year period we must deal not only with styles, but also with the men who dreamed them up. Recognising furniture by the yardstick of reigns is all right up to this point; so far we have cheerfully accepted 'William and Mary', 'Queen Anne' and 'Early Georgian': now we meet the four un-crowned Kings of Design.

High-class Chippendale chair

The Big Four are Thomas Chippendale, Robert Adam (and his brother James), George Hepplewhite and Thomas Sheraton: designers, creators

13

Simpler Chippendale chair

of fashion, trend-setters of enormous influence. These are the men whose names appear in auction catalogues and on tickets attached to the most expensive antique furniture—'A fine set of Hepplewhite dining chairs', 'a magnificent Chippendale chest of drawers, 1755'—enough to frighten an expert, let alone you and me. Although only a fraction of period furniture can actually be attributed to one or another of these top workshops, a basic knowledge of each of the four styles is crucial; so let's take it slowly, first noting some points which often cause confusion.

There is no clear-cut division in time between the four men and their work. Adam overlaps with Chippendale, Hepplewhite with Adam, and Sheraton with Hepplewhite *and* Adam—think of a relay race, except that here every man has his own stick and they all keep running. If you want to know how intricate the overlapping of styles can be, read the next paragraph. If you don't, don't.

Chippendale was making a name for himself by about 1745; his influence was probably at its height between 1754 and 1770. Yet during the 1760's, concurrently with the Chippendale vogue, the Adam brothers designed furniture with an entirely different 'look': their creations were intended as accessories to the classical revival in architecture promoted by Adam during this time. Adam furniture rivalled Chippendale's for prominence in fashion, and Adam influence remained strong to the end of the 18th century. Hepplewhite, too, had a long run for his money. Primarily a designer of chairs, he probably designed and made mahogany ones as early as the mid-1760's, and after his death his firm carried on to produce the painted chairs advertised in his 'Guide' in 1788–89. Characteristics of the 'Hepplewhite style' apply to both types. With Adam and Hepplewhite fashions still in full swing, Sheraton must have been pressed for original ideas when he published his 'Drawing Book' of furniture in 1791–his designs demonstrate considerable brain-picking. But although he borrowed the fragile look begun by Adam and continued by Hepplewhite, and also the idea of painting his furniture, he had a definite 'look' and style of his own.

It is all very complicated. The final word on the Big Four is even more complicated, but we'll save that up until we have coped with the details.

Chippendale characteristics

(a) The curved cresting rail we saw on the Early Georgian chair continues in the cupid's bow or 'serpentine' outline, now more pronounced.

(b) The earlier pierced splat now opens out to fill more of the back space. It can be carved in an open-work strap design, like the one in the picture, or in a specific pattern: the *Ladder Back*, which was very popular; the *Ribband Back*, a fashionable back for really classy chairs; the *Chinese lattice Back* or the *Gothic Back*, both of which are now rare and precious.

(c) Straight, square-section legs joined by stretchers come back to fashion for the first time since Stuart days, but don't be surprised to find the cabriole leg still around, maybe ending in a simple scroll foot. Chippendale seldom used the claw-and-ball foot on his own work, but his many disciples kept it going, and you are more likely to find it than the scrolled foot.

(d) Upholstered chair backs are square and plain.

(e) The Chippendale-style chair combines handsomeness with strength. Plain carved mahogany suits the style, and there are no frills. It is a practical, masculine piece of furniture.

'Country Chippendale' chair

Adam chair

(f) 'Country Chippendale' simply means early second-rate Chippendale: simpler, country-made adaptations of high-fashion examples. The splat piercing is not nearly so elaborate; the legs are straight and plain; the seat is often plain wood, and the wood itself may not be mahogany, but oak or a fruit-wood. These have not been copied at all, whereas stylish models have been reproduced without number, so any you see will be antique, if impossible to date accurately.

Adam characteristics

(a) This is a very different type of chair from anything we have seen so far: the lines are delicate and elegant and the structure is very much lighter.

15

(b) Chair backs can be round, square, oval or shield-shaped; upholstered backs are usually oval.

(c) The legs are straight, slim and tapering, with no stretchers; they are often fluted in the manner of classical columns.

(d) The Adam brothers were the first to go wild over surface decoration: their chairs are gilded and painted, and often veneered in light-coloured woods such as satin wood or tulip wood.

(e) The decoration takes the form of classical motifs galore: *urns*, round and oval *medallions, vases*, festoons of flowers and drapery, rows of small leaves, and sometimes animal heads.

(f) The Adam chair is feminine in the Greek goddess tradition— slender, elegant, cool; certainly not the type to treat casually. Old copies are fairly few and far between, and they are likely to be pretty dear as second-rate chairs go. The real thing can be unbelievably expensive—although Adam influence was important in furniture design of the later 18th century, his actual style was quickly displaced by Hepplewhite and Sheraton, so there are not many genuine pieces which can be dated to his period of fashion.

Hepplewhite characteristics

(a) This chair style is not as 'stand-offish' as Adam's, although the general idea is the same: light, graceful and curvy.

(b) The back is very important: it is very much lower than the Chippendale chair back, and rather lower than the Adam back; the outline can be oval, heart-shaped, wheel-shaped (with a central spoke filling) or a plain rounded hoop similar to the Queen Anne back line, containing a carved open-work splat. The *shield-shaped back* (as shown in the picture) was first used by Adam but is always associated with the Hepplewhite style.

Hepplewhite shield-back chair

(c) The back filling can be a carved splat or a specific design: the *lyre splat*, urn, the *wheat-ear* motif, classical draperies, or the *three ostrich* feathers symbol of the Prince of Wales.

(d) Legs may be square or cylindrical, and occasionally a slim curved 'French-style' *cabriole* appears. They all taper, but straight legs taper only on the inside.

(e) Square legs sometimes end in a *spade foot*, but during the later 18th century the *thimble foot* becomes popular for both round and square legs.

(f) Decoration follows the classical scheme first exploited by Adam: medallions, chains of flowers, fluting, little strings of petals and leaves. Whether carved, moulded or inlaid, the ornament is very delicate and refined.

(g) Two Hepplewhite clues illustrated here are the gap between the back filling and the seat frame; and the small half-hoop at the base of the back filling itself.

(h) The arms of armchairs and sofas curve in one smooth sweep from the back uprights to the front of the seat, instead of the usual armrest supported by a short upright rising from the front of the seat frame.

(i) The Hepplewhite style is a tricky one—there are so many alternatives. Watch for the shield back, the tapered leg and some form of back design: maybe a simple carved splat. Hepplewhite's many followers did not necessarily keep to the straight and narrow path of the master drawings, and they often found the painting-and-gilding vogue too demanding on their talents or perhaps too expensive for their less fashionable clients. We are more likely to find Hepplewhite-style chairs in carved mahogany or perhaps rosewood.

Sheraton Characteristics

(a) Sheraton was an upright man, and he saw no reason why chairs should be otherwise. He must have thought that Hepplewhite's curves were positively abandoned: after nearly a century of curvy furniture we find that Sheraton revives the straight line.

(b) Chair backs are square or nearly square, with straight, horizontal top and bottom rails. The gap between the seat and the back is borrowed from Hepplewhite.

(e) Many back fillings emphasise straight lines: parallel uprights evenly spaced apart; or grouped into a central splat arrangement. Sheraton also uses the three-feather motif first designed by Hepplewhite, the wheatear, and the Adam-style vase, festoons of drapery and other classical emblems in his decoration.

(d) Sheraton legs taper, and they may be round or square section. '*Reeding*' becomes popular for all furniture legs. The thimble foot alternates with the *peg-top foot* (this returns to popularity on Victorian chairs).

(e) The chair outline may be severe, but Sheraton decoration is the daintiest, prettiest style in English furniture ornament. He went to town on wreaths of flowers, knots of ribbon, garlands of leaves, slim vases, tassels, baskets of blossoms and posies, painted and inlaid with the greatest care for detail and colour.

(f) 'Inlay' is very nearly synonymous with 'Sheraton': dark

wood inlay on a light wood chair, or light wood inlaid in dark wood. We are not very likely to find much painted work in our price range, but the many Sheraton copies around usually have some inlay—or decoration painted to look like inlay.

(g) Chair arms do not curve as Hepplewhite arms do: Sheraton returns to the vertical upright from the seat to support the arm rest.

(h) The Sheraton chair is a remarkable combination of severity and fuss—like a mannequin parading in a tailored suit and the prettiest, floweriest hat imaginable.

The Final Word

In spite of this mass of bewildering detail the antique chairs that we are concerned with will be only approximate replicas of one or another of the four master styles. Worse: many chairs in this second-rate category will be mongrels, hybrid combinations of features gleaned from two, three, or even all four styles. Thus you might run across a chair with Chippendale-style square section legs and stretchers, a Hepplewhite-style shield back, perhaps some Sheraton-style inlay, and carved classical motifs à la Adam. If you

consider the chair back the most significant pointer of style, you can call the piece 'Hepplewhite' and few people will be any the wiser. The important thing is to know what you are getting: if you like the chair, buy it; if you don't, count the different characteristics and leave it alone. But the more closely a piece of antique furniture resembles the original design, the more expensive it is likely to be.

About 1800-1830

Regardless of historical fact, this period of English furniture is known as 'Regency': from here on our price range might embrace an original or two. Chairs of this particular period style were very much influenced by post-French Revolution fashions: a wave of designs inspired by the furniture of Ancient Greece, Rome and Egypt swept across the Channel to England; and the first few years of the 19th century

'Mongrel' chair

saw a radical change in the appearance of upper-class drawing rooms. The style is neo-classical, but not at all like the delicate, fragile classical revival of the later 18th century. The Regency translation of the classics is a much more weighty, ponderous work than the gilded grace of Adam's interpretation: 'An ordinary chair, in the most ordinary parlour . . . has something of Grecian massiveness', Sir Walter Scott remarked with approval. Ordinary chairs in ordinary parlours are just up the non-collector's street, and this is what they look like.

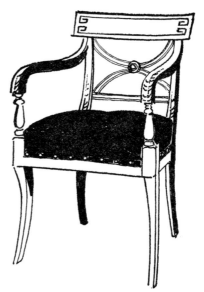

Early Regency chair

(a) Chairs may be of mahogany or rosewood; painted and gilded chairs were made for the more fashionable market, but plain carved wood is more in our line.

(b) The back is fairly low: it tends to be square, and the back top rail often curls over backwards.

(c) The legs are important: the front legs curve forwards in the shape of a curved sword—a '*sabre*' or '*scimitar*', and the back legs do the same in the opposite direction.

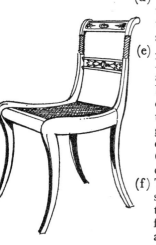

(d) The arms of arm chairs are rather high up; they usually curve down from the level of the top of the back uprights to end in a scroll supported by scrolled uprights rising from the seat frame.

(e) *Brass inlay* in the wood is a characteristic of Regency furniture decoration in general, and appears on chairs at all price levels. Besides brass inlay, you will see a lot of antiquarian ornament on expensive pieces: Egyptian heads, the bearded face of Bacchus, lyres, winged lions, griffins, the Sphinx, lion heads and many dragons and mock pagodas in a revival of the Chinese taste which swept through Regency drawing rooms like Asian 'flu.

(f) The sabre-legged Regency chair is comfortable, stable and meant to be sat on. The plainer it is the more adaptable it will be to the rest of your furniture, and if you look hard you should be able to find the genuine article at a reasonable cost. Reproductions are legion, but it should not be too difficult to avoid those which were

Regency chair

19

clearly made the day before yesterday; late 19th and early 20th century ones are less self-consciously phony and usually much better-made.

Victorian Chairs

The long, long reign of Victoria (1837–1901) is studded with a bewildering variety of chairs: if you want information about them all you must look elsewhere, for here it is possible to catalogue only a few. There is no tidy sequence of styles as there is in the 18th century: many different styles marched relentlessly into Victorian dining rooms and parlours as the weathercock of fashion shifted around the points of the 19th century; today they march out of attics and auctions into modern homes. The Balloon-back, the Buttoned-back and a word or two about reproductions should cover enough ground to satisfy the average non-collecting consumer with conservative tastes, and this is what they look like:

Victorian balloon-back chair

Balloon-back Chair

The balloon-back style came into fashion after the first few years of the reign and continued to be made pretty steadily till the end of the 19th century, though by then its tremendous popularity was well on the wane. If any one chair style can be called 'typically Victorian', this is the one.

(a) The back uprights of the chair curve towards each other near the bottom, then puff out and up to form a smooth oval back outline. A curved, often decorated cross rail supports the middle of the sitter's back and completes the oval 'balloon', leaving a considerable gap between it and the back of the seat frame.

(b) The front legs can be straight, turned in various shapes, or they may be the slim, graceful 'French cabriole'. The back legs are plain and splay out slightly.

(c) The seat may be the 'drop-in' type, or upholstered all over. Balloon-backed chairs with cabriole legs usually have curvy seat-frames; straight-legged models have straight frames.

(d) Balloon-backs may be mahogany or rosewood, and they are probably the most comfortable straight chair around. The

20

oval back curves to fit the shoulders and the cross rail supports your spine just where it needs supporting. And, in spite of everything you hear about ornate Victorian furniture, this style is not: the front legs and the cross rail may be decoratively carved, but that's all; and you'll find that they mix well with almost anything. You might have trouble finding a matched set of half-a-dozen, but it should be easy to accumulate a near-miss set if the back heights are the same and the leg styles tally—anyway, odd lots of two or three chairs come much cheaper.

'French-style' cabriole leg ending in a peg-top foot

Button-backs

Button-back sofas and easy chairs have the upholstery fixed with buttons sunk into the thick padding, emphasising the lush, comfortable curves. This was a rave fashion during the first half of Victoria's reign and there are any number of examples to choose from, particularly low-seated easy chairs, with or without arms, on short, curvy, cabriole-type legs. The upholstered back is often 'spoon-shaped'—this looks like a higher, solid version of the open balloon-back—and armless models often have a wooden frame around the curvy back outline. These chairs are cheap to buy and can look very elegant in the living room—or in a bedroom, where they add that boudoir tone cultivated by cosmetic advertisements and young brides. Those with arms are more comfortable than those without: somehow the low, armless ones make it difficult for you to cross your legs and you are left with your knees nearly on a level with your nose. If you go in for long housecoats and hostess gowns, though, these easy chairs make graceful, lady-like seats, particularly if you bring your embroidery along. Just don't expect a man to look happy in them; and remember that re-upholstering a beaten-up bargain can cost five times what you paid in the first place.

Victorian button-back chair

21

Reproductions

The late-Victorian period is the starting point of the Age of Reproductions. Good quality copies of 18th century furniture designs were made throughout the 19th century, and Elizabethan, Grecian, Gothic and Louis XV-French copies were modish in the 1830's and 40's, but in the 1870's the demand for Chippendale-, Adam-, Hepplewhite- and Sheraton-style furniture was stepped up. Reproductions became a definite vogue, and remained so to the end of the century and on into the Edwardian era.

If you look at the history of Victorian furniture in more detail you will see that the late-19th century passion for 18th century design represented a desperate desire to raise the standard of taste, which by the 1860's had fallen to an all-time low. Up to, say, the Great Exhibition of 1851, the Victorians were addled by a hectic search for novelty: different materials, techniques and styles crowded one upon the other in frantic haste and, in the exhilaration of the moment, good taste got left behind and forgotten. As a result, the 1850's and 60's are a nightmare of fussy ornamentation indicating a lack of good design. The more ornament, the more beauty, was the cabinet-maker's slogan: furniture was smothered with carving and every form of decoration known to man. The 1870's saw the beginning of the reaction to this; as yet design was too bogged down to go forward, but it did go back, and luckily it went back to the designs of an age when good taste was all-important.

Chairs, and other pieces in the style of the 18th century masters, which look old, yet are accurately styled and reasonably priced, are likely to be Victorian-made. The price is your best guide; but only an expert could tell the difference between an 18th century Chippendale original and a high class 19th century copy which by now has mellowed so as to be almost indistinguishable from the genuine article and is priced accordingly. There are any amount of standard Victorian reproductions in the second-rate antique trade, and this should be borne in mind as you battle through the rest of this book. They are the antiques which are not really antique, the fakes, the phonies with machine-carved decoration finished by hand, the inlay painted on instead of inlaid, the wood stained to look like mahogany or satinwood. The more nearly a piece resembles the first-rate original, the more likely it is to be a Victorian or Edwardian copy—unless you see it in a very smart antique shop or in a museum, in which case you examine it narrowly and then tip-toe respectfully away.

Chapter 3

Tables Great and Small

TABLES are of two basic kinds: those which, when you sit down for dinner, put their legs just where you want to put yours; and the other kind—exactly low enough for you to bark your shins. Apart from dining and coffee tables, whose function is usually obvious, antique table-talk includes a lot of tables with specific purposes and fancy names. Although you may buy one for a reason which has nothing in common with the table's original use, it helps to know a few names, particularly as everyone in the business uses them.

To simplify the chaos of combining working definitions with various period styles I have sub-divided tables into three groups: 'Useful Large', 'Useful Small' and 'Decorative Medium'—the last lot to include those tables which have little official use nowadays but which are handy to have around to dump things on. All the tables are dealt with in the order given, and to get an idea of the prevailing fashion in furniture during any particular period you should refer back to the chair whose date corresponds with that of a particular table.

Useful Large	Useful Small	Decorative Medium
Dining tables	Tripod tables	Pembroke tables
Sideboards	Nests of tables	Console tables
Sofa tables	Work tables	Pier tables
Dressing tables		Side tables
Drum tables		Card tables

'Useful Large'

Dining Tables

(a) The *Framed Draw-top* table, usually made of oak, was used as a dining table during the greater part of the 17th century or 'Stuart' period. This is a hefty affair standing on four massive turned legs joined by heavy stretchers near ground level: the stretchers form a rectangle or 'frame'. Two extra leaves lie beneath the table-top proper, and can be pulled out to extend the length—hence 'draw-top'. The legs can be turned in shapes similar to those on chairs of the period, and carved decoration follows the same lines.

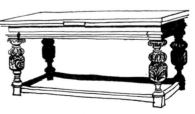

Framed draw-top table

23

Gate-leg table

(b) The *Gate-legged* table gradually replaced the framed draw-top as the table for the new-fangled dining room, fashionable in houses after about 1660. Gate-leg tables were made first of oak, later of walnut: they remained popular right through Queen Anne's reign and up to about 1720; and they have been copied ad infinitum since then. The top consists of an oblong centre board with a hinged flap on either side. The raised flaps are supported by pairs of legs, each pair joined by stretchers, which swing out from the centre as a garden gate swings on its hinges. The table top can be round or oval, and the leg shapes are usually slimmer versions of framed draw-top table legs, though a popular design is a *twisted 'barley-sugar'* form. The gate-leg style of table was originally a large dining model, but it comes in all sizes, so don't be surprised to see them.

(c) The mahogany *Flap Dining table* is the prototype for many such tables over the last 200-odd years. It replaced the gate-leg in fashionable Early Georgian dining rooms between about 1720 and the mid-1750's. The hinged flap extension is based on the same principle as the earlier model, but the legs do not follow the 'swinging gate' shape: instead a single cabriole leg with a club foot swings out to support each flap by means of a concealed wooden 'fly' bracket beneath the table top. Stretchers are discarded altogether; and the fixed legs supporting the centre board are cabriole also. The complete table top can be round or oval; a medium-sized table stands on four legs; larger ones can have six or even eight.

(d) The *Chippendale-style dining table* of the 1750's follows the same lines as the previous style: mahogany; fully-opened round or oval top; hinged flaps with single leg supports. The legs alone reflect the fashion of the day: they may be cabriole ending in carved claw-and-ball feet, or straight in square section (See Chippendale-style chairs).

(e) The much lighter style of dining table which appeared during the 1760's links up with the graceful chair designs of *Adam*, *Hepplewhite* and *Sheraton*. The slim, tapered legs are fixed, for there are no flaps to support, and in fact the complete table is made up from four small tables placed together to form one big one: two oblong middle sections and two semi-circular ends which can be separate duty as sidetables. Don't break your heart hunting for a complete foursome: most examples have long since been split up, and those that haven't are likely to be wildly expensive, including 19th century copies. Anyway,

Regency dining table

19th century reproductions 'in the Adam, Hepplewhite or Sheraton style' are usually simple oval or rectangular tables with later-18th-century-style legs and decoration, and made in one piece. They may not be accurate copies of the original idea, but so what? It's the food that counts, after all.

(f) *Regency* dining tables of the early 19th century are weighty pieces in mahogany or rosewood. They follow the neo-classical fashion, but are very different from the delicate lines of late 18th century furniture. The round or oval table top is supported by a massive central pillar with 3 or 4 claw feet on brass castors. Another version comes in sections: rectangular boards on pillars with splayed legs similar to Regency chair 'sabre' legs. These sections fit or clip together, and the table can be extended to any length.

(g) Most *Victorian* dining tables are rectangular, standing on four fat turned legs. The ends may be square or rounded, and the table can be extended with extra leaves. Some might be carved after the manner of Tudor and Stuart tables. Circular dining tables may have extra slips of wood, triangular-shaped, to extend the circumference, but this sort was not as common as the rectangular model.

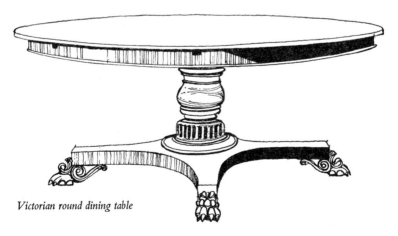

Victorian round dining table

Sideboards

The one-piece side-board as we know it, with drawers and cup-boards, is an invention of the later 18th century, though Side-tables (see 'Decorative Medium') were used as serving tables or sideboards from a much earlier date. The design familiar nowadays may have originated with Hepplewhite, or perhaps a contemporary of his called Thomas Shearer. At any rate, it deserves a mention on its own.

(a) The *Hepplewhite-style* sideboard has a straight front, a bow-shaped front, or the serpentine-shaped outline—the bow-front is more common. Across the front is a long shallow drawer for table linen, and below it two cupboards or more drawers. Straight-fronted sideboards have four tapered square-section legs ending in thimble feet; a curved-fronted model may have four legs in the front and two at the back. The wood is usually mahogany, sometimes decorated with inlay in paler wood.

(b) The *Sheraton-style* sideboard is very similar to the above: serpentine or bow-front; drawers and cupboards. The legs are usually turned, rather than square-section, and they are often carved or reeded. A low brass rail or 'gallery' runs across the back on some examples, to support plates and salvers.

(c) *Victorian* sideboards can be incredibly ornate, with carved backs and mirrors to reflect the family collection of decanters and wine-bottles. They are also incredibly large, so be sure you have enough space before you buy one. One day they may become very O.K. period pieces; today they are just a nuisance, but at least a cheap nuisance.

Late 18th century sideboard

Sofa Tables

The upholstered padded sofa (as opposed to the double- or triple-chair settee) became popular in the late 18th and early 19th century. The mahogany or rosewood sofa table was a fashionable piece in Regency and Victorian parlours, as a reading and writing table for ladies sitting on sofas, relaxing on sofas, or otherwise sofa-occupied. It is a larger edition of the Pembroke table (see Decorative Medium): a rectangular table with a hinged flap at each end, supported when raised by wooden 'fly' brackets. There is sometimes a drawer or two in the underframe below the central table-board; and the table stands on four legs or alternatively on two curved bracket legs joined together by a stretcher. 19th century examples often stand on a central column resting on a flat platform with curved sabre-type legs.

Dressing Tables

(a) During the late *Stuart* period (about 1660–1690) small oak or walnut tables with two or three drawers in the front were used as dressing tables. They were used as writing tables too, but we won't bother about that—they're not desks as such, and if you deal in such riddles as 'when is a desk not a desk?' the answer is a dressing table. Many have hinged flaps and gate-leg supports; and some have turned baluster legs like dining tables of the day.

(b) *The Queen Anne and Early Georgian* dressing (or writing) table is easier to recognise as such. It has a 'kneehole' front, with two or three drawers on either side of the gap and perhaps one drawer across the top, which may open up to show a hinged mirror, and several little compartments below it. The

Dressing-table-cum-kneehole desk

top is about three feet wide, and the legs are cabriole, with plain club feet. Walnut or mahogany, by the way, and very expensive.

(c) The *Chippendale-style* model is an extension of the above: a mahogany table with a long top drawer containing little compartments and a hinged mirror. Sometimes the top lifts up to show the fitted interior underneath. The central kneehole is now often filled with a cupboard, with two or three drawers down either side, and the table stands on six bracket feet: two at the back, and four square- or *ogee*-shaped feet in front.

(d) The *Hepplewhite-style* dressing table is, for the first time in the ambidextrous history of the piece, a dressing table only. The front can be straight, bow-shaped or serpentine shaped; there are several drawers in several sizes; and the kneehole gap, while not so obvious as the earlier 18th century examples, is still worthy of the name. An adjustable mirror on a swivel is fixed at each side of the top, and the middle of the top lifts up as another mirror, with a range of fittings in the first layer of the chest. This late 18th century model usually comes in mahogany, with slim bracket feet curving out at the bottom.

(e) The *Regency-style* dressing table can be mahogany, rosewood, or satinwood; it is a heavier piece than the elegant Hepplewhite

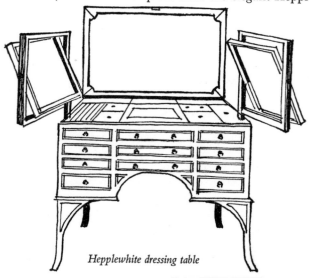

Hepplewhite dressing table

representative, standing on two columns ending in splayed scrolled feet, or sometimes four short legs, with no columns. The straight front has three drawers, or two deeper ones, with a low shelf below them.

(f) *Victorian* dressing tables come in all sorts of woods and all sorts of styles; pedestal, kneehole, sometimes just a chest of drawers with fitted mirrors. They are large and heavy, sometimes lavishly and hideously carved, but at least they do a useful job—more so than some of the modern frilly ones you see today. You'll know them when you see them, anyway.

Drum Tables

Drum table

These were common in the early 19th century: large round tables in mahogany or rosewood, standing either on a hefty three-sided pedestal with claw feet, or on a slimmer pedestal with curved sabre-shaped legs. Victorian and Edwardian reproductions often have tooled leather tops, but you are not likely to see leather on originals. The catch about these tables is their multiplicity of names: 'Library table' or 'Capstan table' are common alternatives to 'Drum'. They sometimes have turning tops, and the deep frieze below the table top contains drawers and/or fake drawer fronts. Library tables proper have drawers containing hinged book rests, so if you run across this type, 'Library table' is the official name. 'Drum', though, will usually do for the rest. If you don't happen to have a library handy in your house, these tables make practically indestructible occasional tables, if difficult to shift around.

'Useful Small'

Tripod Tables

These small occasional tables littered fashionable drawing rooms from the early Georgian period onwards. The round top rests on a slim central standard supported by three legs—hence the 'tripod'. The table top is often hinged, so that it can be tipped to a vertical position and placed against the wall out of the way. They are usually found in mahogany; occasionally satinwood or rosewood, and the many 19th century reproductions can be anything from walnut to papier mâché and wrought iron.

The *Chippendale-style* model has cabriole legs with claw-and-ball, club, or paw feet; the table top is plain or wavy-edged, sometimes fitted with a carved gallery or railing, or with the well-known '*pie-crust*'

29

Tripod table

decoration round the rim (though both these additions are a sure sign of the first-rate price bracket).

The *Adam-Hepplewhite-Sheraton* tripod table has slimmer feet than the earlier design, and the central support can be vase-shaped. Really good examples may have a pierced gallery round the top, but plain tables are more common, and these may have simple pad feet, or peg-feet turning inward. This late 18th century style is lighter and more graceful than the preceding Chippendale-style or the following Regency model.

Regency tripod tables have sabre legs with splayed-out feet. The basic design remains the same.

Nests of Tables

Sets of three ('trio') or four ('quartetto') little tables became very fashionable during the early 19th century as occasional tea or coffee tables. They are usually mahogany or rosewood; the smaller sizes fit into and underneath the larger ones, like Chinese boxes; and sometimes the legs are *'spindled'*—a simpler, streamlined variation of the turned legs and uprights common on Stuart chairs.

Work Tables

Work tables were introduced in the 1760's as work-boxes-cum-writing stands for fashionable ladies in fashionable boudoirs. Early examples, usually in satinwood, are more elegant than serviceable (Sheraton designed some beauties); but Regency and Victorian models in mahogany or rosewood are sturdier—and a lot less expensive.

Designs vary slightly: the basic idea is a wooden box about

Victorian work table

30

18 inches square by 9 inches or a foot deep, standing on slender supports or a central pillar, and about two and a half feet high. The front of the box may drop down on hinges to act as a small desk flap or sewing top; the tray-top lifts up to show the well for sewing or writing things, or alternatively a fabric bag hanging inside and below the wooden box-frame, like the illustration model. Alternative box-frame styles are round or hexagonal, and the top may be chequered for playing draughts or chess.

Sheraton-style supports consist of two slender legs, each on a "bracket' of two feet curving downwards back and front, and joined together by a horizontal stretcher. Regency work tables often stand on the pillar-and-claw base popular for other tables of the period; and Victorian examples may follow any and all of the previous styles.

'Decorative Medium'

Pembroke Tables

Pembroke tables or, as Chippendale called them, 'breakfast' tables, have remained the same in style and popularity for two hundred years. The full top can be oval or rectangular, and the size is neither big nor small—handy for breakfast, or tea, or a dinner à deux, as you feel inclined. If you want a hall table there is enough space for dumping gloves, hats and letters; and if your criterion is not utility you can rest assured that the Pembroke table looks nice just standing around doing nothing.

The main board is about 3 to 4 feet by 1½ to 2 feet wide, with a drawer in the frieze at each end, across the width. A flap, supported by a swinging 'fly' bracket, is hinged to each *long* side of the top: when the table is fully *Pembroke table* extended it is perhaps 4 to 6 feet long.

The *Chippendale-style* Pembroke table is rectangular, with straight, square-section legs joined by X-stretchers.

The *late 18th century* style often has an oval top, though rectangular tops stay in fashion, and the legs follow the slim tapered lines of Adam-Hepplewhite-Sheraton chair-legs. Stretchers disappear; and veneered or painted satinwood is as much in vogue as the plainer mahogany.

The *Regency-style* Pembroke table is supported by the pillar-and-claw method used for other tables of the period. Oval tops are commoner than rectangular ones.

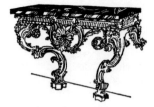

Console Tables

'Console', originally 'clap', is a fancy name for those side tables which rest against the wall and have two front legs only. They appeared first in the early 18th century, often with heavy marble tops and very ornate, carved and gilded underframes and legs. Elongated eagles, dolphins and fantastic monsters vied for popularity with the cabriole leg as supports: the style of ornament is right outside the mainstream of plain, understated furniture and leans heavily and elaborately towards the extravaganzas of early and mid-18th century France. Later examples are lighter in appearance: the slim, tapering leg and classical motif decoration link up with the disciplined lines of Adam, Hepplewhite and Sheraton furniture; but Regency console tables return to the very elaborate over-weight style as before.

The real thing seems to be a collector's dream; and even copies are likely to be over-priced, but if you like grand, fussy furniture, console tables are all yours.

Pier Tables

The 'pier' is that part of the wall between two windows. Pier tables were fashionable throughout the 18th century, designed to stand in just that very space below a 'Pier glass'—a narrow mirror in an elaborate frame (see Whatnots: Mirrors). The style is very much like the console table; ornately decorated with carving and gilding, often with a marble top which can be D-shaped, serpentine-fronted, or rectangular; but the pier table has four legs, not two, and Sheraton-style examples may have graceful stretchers. Legs vary according to the current vogue: the most elegant are those associated with the great designers of the late 18th century. If you have neither a 'pier' against which to place a pier table, nor a pier glass to hang above it, you could call it a 'four-legged console table' and put it wherever you like. It's strictly a decoration piece, though.

Side Tables

The very term 'side' is the vaguest definition in the dictionary of antique jargon. Practically any table can become a side table by the simple expedient of putting it beside a wall, but for those of us who are sticklers for the facts, there are two basic types of side table proper, and here they are.

First: those tables used as serving tables before the invention of the sideboard (see Useful Large) were known as 'side tables'.

Second: those well-known, well-loved, useless tables like the pier and the console, designed to take up about 18 square feet of space while holding one vase of flowers, can be called side tables when you can't remember their official names: 'side' is a fair substitute and there's no need to feel guilty. If, however, you are the type who could pick a pier table from a console in the middle of an eclipse, and you see a table that you know isn't either, then it's a side table pure and simple.

(a) *Late 17th and early 18th century* side tables were usually made of carved walnut, with heavy carved legs joined by scrolled X-stretchers meeting at a central knob, or plainer stretchers in 'H' formation. The underframe or frieze beneath the table top sometimes contains a drawer. Another type of this period has a folding top supported by two swinging front legs. Leg designs correspond with chair legs of the late Stuart and William-and-Mary style.

(b) *Early Georgian* side tables have marble or imitation marble tops about 5 or 6 feet long, with massive, lavishly gilded underframes. The legs are cabriole, ornately decorated with carving and gilding.

(c) Plainer side tables were popular for a short time after 1740. These can have marble tops like the earlier tables (mahogany-topped models were used as sideboards) but the underframes and cabriole legs are simply carved and mercifully innocent of gilding.

(d) The *Chippendale-style* side table of the 1750's often has square-section legs with the inner edges smoothed flat—pared off to make the line more elegant.

(e) *Adam-style* side tables can be gilded and painted, or plain mahogany delicately carved with the neo-classical motifs popular from the 1760's on. The table top can be marble, and the legs are slim, tapered, and sometimes reeded like classical columns. This type of table became a 'sideboard table' when flanked by two separate pedestals in matching style: one of these was fitted out as a platewarmer, the other as a knife-case or a cellaret; and each carried an urn or vase for water. These sideboard groups of three were still cluttering up 18th century dining rooms when the one-piece sideboard, with drawers and cupboards, finally appeared. It seems so obvious now—and the *Hepplewhite-Sheraton* piece has been widely copied in preference to the side-table-and-pedestals group—but these hair-splitting definitions are necessary, to clear up the very natural confusion of the non-expert buyer.

(f) *Regency* side tables are ponderous affairs in mahogany or rosewood, rather similar to those made early in the 18th century. 19th century decoration, however, favoured carved lions, and brass ornament; and the supports are often pillar-and-claw style.

Card Tables

(a) During the later *17th century* cards were a very popular pastime, but as yet no specific card table had evolved: gate-legged tables or side tables, covered with a cloth, did duty as card tables when required.

(b) The reigns of *William and Mary and Queen Anne* coincided with a passion for gambling which raged in the world of fashion for more than 100 years. Cards became more than a mild diversion: they dominated the smart social scene to an extraordinary extent; the card table market began to boom; and designs multiplied throughout the 18th century. If you have an original, treat it with respect—fortunes may have been made and unmade across that table top.

The first table top design as such appeared about 1700. The folding top can be circular, or about 3 feet square with rounded projecting corners: the hinged semi-circular or rectangular flap lifts up to rest on one, and sometimes two back legs, which swing out to support it. An adaptation of this table is the 'concertina' type: the flap rests on a hinged, folding underframe, which pulls out from beneath the main half-table top in expanding concertina fashion, with two legs fixed to it. Yet another type of the same period is a triangular table opening to a square. All three styles of card table have the cabriole leg, usually ending in a club foot; and the shell motif may be carved on the knee, like Queen Anne chair legs. These tables were originally made in walnut, but have been copied in mahogany and other woods.

Card table

(c) *Early Georgian* card tables can be mahogany or walnut, and have projecting, squared-off corners to the table top. Really good examples have a serpentine-shaped outline, and more carved decoration on the cabriole legs—such extras put up the price enormously. Claw-and-ball, and scroll feet have come into vogue, but the plain club or pad foot is still around.

(d) The *Chippendale-style* card table is very like the earlier one: the cabriole leg remains popular, and the claw-and-ball foot becomes common; but legs can now be straight, and square-section. One movable back leg supports the folding half-top. High quality pieces may have carving around the top edge and on the frieze.

(e) Card tables in the style of *Hepplewhite or Sheraton* can be circular or square, with straight, tapering legs in either round or square section, often ending in little club feet. The fashion for light, elegant, painted or veneered satinwood furniture produced most beautiful tables for society gambling rooms, clubs and salons—expensive then and expensive now, and copies seem to be few and far between.

(f) *Regency* card tables can be mahogany or rosewood, often with inlaid decoration in brass or in a contrasting wood. The top may be square, on tapered legs with curved-out feet; or resting on four shorter legs which in turn stand on a small central platform on short sabre legs. Alternatively the top may be D-shaped opening to an approximate circle, resting on the Regency-style pillar-and-claws base. Regency examples might be within our price range, but originals of earlier card tables can be wickedly expensive, particularly those of high quality. Still, a safari into country districts might yield a prize in the form of an old, simply-made copy.

That covers most of the tables you are likely to want in your house. Not all: you will probably see all sorts and conditions of tables not dealt with here—wine tables, perhaps, and urn tables, and heaven knows what Victorian eccentricities. If you can whip up the enthusiasm to find out more about them, buy another antique book. Or try a little guesswork.

Chapter 4

Desks and more Desks

THE telephone, we are often told, dealt the death blow to the art of letter-writing; and the typewriter slammed the nails into its coffin. Be that as it may, letters still have to be written, and if you are more likely to get inspiration staring at antique pigeon-holes, rather than at the spattered wall above the kitchen table, you should buy some writing paper and start from here.

There are two kinds of desk: 'Business-like' and 'Lady-like'. Business-like examples run from medium sized family desks to the huge pieces of antique tycoonery in chairmen's offices; but since we are not concerned with the grandest sort of anything, you will find here only those business-like desks of less than executive size—they have room for the normal family accumulation of bills, insurance policies, school reports, photographs and empty ink bottles, but they don't make you feel that children's bread-and-butter letters are beneath their dignity.

Lady-like desks are small, elegant affairs for writing small elegant notes beginning: 'Lady de Winter presents her compliments . . .'' in a fine calligraphic hand. Like many elegant ladies, these desks tend to be very expensive and not very useful around the house; but since a great many housewives cherish this very image as their ultimate aim in life, the purchase of a tiny satinwood writing table may be the first step along the stony way. Most are Sheraton or Sheraton-inspired; and while there are many permutations on the basic lady-like scheme, only a few are included here.

'Business-like'

Bureau Desk

This is the Mark One model of the family desk: sturdy, useful, and probably the best loved of the lot. It is the first desk proper, displacing the portable writing boxes and numerous indeterminate tables used as desks up to the end of the 17th century.

(a) The basic style is generally known as 'Queen Anne'. It is between two and three feet wide: the bottom stage contains two or three long drawers and two short ones; and the piece stands on short, squarish feet. The upper, or writing section has a sloping front which swings down as a writing surface, supported by pull-out struts beside the two top drawers. This slope-front covers a fitted interior of small drawers, pigeon-holes, a small central cupboard; and sometimes a false bottom with two or three secret hidey-holes. Early 18th century examples were usually made in walnut; later on mahogany became very popular, but you will find them in oak, rosewood, pine, and various other woods.

(b) *Chippendale* produced beautiful bureaux like this in mahogany, with fittings and linings of mahogany or oak, and elegantly-curved brass loop drawer handles. Second-rate copies of these are common, some dating from the 18th century, and while the size may vary the style does not. Prices depend on age, condition, and general quality of construction; but if you want a useful, handsome desk you could hardly do better.

(e) Both Hepplewhite and Sheraton designed their own variations on the bureau desk theme, but the Queen Anne model continued at the hands of less fashionable craftsmen through-

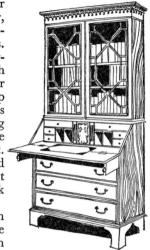

Bureau bookcase

out the later 18th century. You may find some with late-18th century features of decoration: a little satinwood inlay around the drawers and on the slope front; circular brass drawer handles, and so on, and such points will tell you that the craftsmen admired Hepplewhite as much as Chippendale. Feet can vary, too: they may be short and tapered, or the more typical curved-bracket shape of the Hepplewhite style; but fervent disciples of Chippendale stuck to the squat, squarish foot of earlier days.

Bureau Bookcase

This means just what it says: a bureau desk with a bookcase on top of it. The bookcase stands nearly as high again as the desk, but it is slightly narrower across and only as deep as the top of the desk's fitted interior. Chippendale loved this piece and designed some superb specimens in mahogany. Strictly speaking, the bookcase doors should be glazed with looking-glass or else should be plain wood, but most reproductions have doors glazed in plain glass in a tracery design. You might find some carved decoration, or a curly *pediment* on top of the *cornice*, but a simply-carved frieze around the top is usually the only frill on a second-rate piece. The feet on the lower desk are squat and square, like those on the Queen Anne bureau desk; but Hepplewhite-style bureau-bookcases have sloping, curved-out bracket feet, and the whole piece is inclined to be taller and narrower than the earlier Chippendale-style type. Bands of inlay around the drawers and doors indicate copying of later 18th century features; and a piece may have inlaid motifs on the slopefront, as well as inlaid banding.

Secretaire

The difference between the secretaire and the bureau bookcase as described above is that the secretaire has a vertical flap front, the bureau bookcase a sloping one. If this isn't academic hair-splitting I don't know what is; but you may decide that 'secretaire' is a smarter word and use it for the bureau bookcase as well. The vertical flap style dates from the walnut days of William-and-Mary and the secretaire as such was fairly well-known in the mid-18th century. Hepplewhite may have concentrated on the production of higher, more elegant versions; but on the whole you may take it that the feet, decoration and general appearance follow bureau bookcase fashions of the various periods and have been copied accordingly.

'Dressing Chest and Bookcase'

This is a Chippendale Special—a rare and precious edition of the secretaire designed for use in a gentleman's dressing room. While his lady worried whether the kneehole desk-cum-dressing-table (see Tables: 'Useful Large') in her boudoir was either or both, the gentleman presumably locked himself in his dressing room and sat at his dressing-chest-and-bookcase. There he wrote letters, worried about his business and his bald spot, and probably wondered how the devil he was going to pay for all this furniture. The lower stage may take the form of a kneehole desk with drawers or cupboards down each side of the gap; the upper stage has a vertical flap which lets down as a writing surface, with shelves enclosed by doors above. Don't expect to see many of these, and don't be surprised to find those very highly priced.

Kneehole Desks

Remember the trouble we had identifying early 18th century dressing tables? Here we go again. If you check back you will get an idea of what early kneehole desks looked like—many of them doubled as dressing tables during the greater part of the 18th century, but when the dressing table finally branched out on its own the kneehole desk

Kidney-shaped kneehole desk

proper came into greater prominence. The size and the wood vary, and so does the price, but you should be able to find just what you want: there seem to be a great many good, plain reproductions around in all sizes. A lot of these will be Victorian and Edwardian, and don't be put off by the new-looking leather tops—these are often added when a desk is done up prior to re-sale. Having flat solid tops, kneehole desks stand up to more heavy elbows and typewriter pounding than the bureau desks with flaps can take. Rectangular ones are common, but you may also see oval and kidney-shaped examples.

Kneehole Desk and Bookcase

This was the forerunner of the bureau bookcase: the kneehole model appeared in about 1700, but was not very common then, nor did it catch on as the bureau type did a little later on. The lower stage has the kneehole with a recessed central cupboard and drawers down each side; above is a vertical flap which lets down to show a fitted interior of little pigeon holes and drawers. The bookcase stage, with shelves enclosed by doors, stands on top.

Tallboy Secretaire

If you look under Chests you will find what a tallboy—or more properly a chest-on-chest—looks like. The tallboy secretaire looks just like it; but what gets it into the desk section is the top drawer of the lower stage, which, when opened, has a falling front as a writing surface. The interior of this drawer may contain little compartments. Not a well-known or a common piece of furniture but if you go around opening tallboy drawers for long enough, you might find one.

Bureau Cabinet

If you like to hoard jewellery or small items such as colour slides or marbles, this piece would make a handsome filing cabinet. The lower stage is a chest of drawers; the upper one is a large cabinet entirely filled with small compartments, drawers and pigeon-holes, enclosed by wooden doors. Unfortunately it is likely to be expensive, as large hulking pieces go: 18th century prices were relatively high for bureau cabinets—look at all that finicky work, after all—and today's prices are higher. You would probably do better with one of the other desk-cum-bookcase models and cut down on the collecting.

Cylinder Desk and Bookcase

This a characteristic Sheraton-style piece, a late-18th century development of the simpler bureau bookcase. The lower stage has a 'tambour' front: wooden slats, fixed to a canvas backing, roll up and disappear bchind the desk top to show a fitted interior and a writing surface. Below the sliding-top section is a large cupboard with shelves, enclosed by two doors and guaranteed to get in your way when you finally decide to sit down and write a letter. The bookcase above the desk has glazed doors in a tracery design. Sheraton used satinwood, or mahogany with satinwood inlay for this model; if it were rather smaller I would call the style 'lady-like'.

'Secretary and Bookcase'

Sheraton produced his own type of secretaire under this name: the lower stage has a kneehole with drawers, not the usual cupboard, recessed in the arch; and one large and one smaller cupboard on either side of it, the small ones on top. Above the kneehole, between the two smaller cupboards, is a fake drawer front which falls on a '*quadrant*' as a writing surface, with tiny pigeon-holes and drawers at the back. The upper stage is the usual bookcase, with shelves and enclosing doors.

Carlton House writing tables

The story goes that this type of writing table was first made at the behest of the Prince Regent, later George IV, for Carlton House; but though Prinny was undoubtedly a man of many whims, I wouldn't pin much faith to the authenticity of this one. Whoever thought it up, this D-shaped table had a great vogue between about 1790 and 1820. The curve of the D has a raised superstructure of small drawers and cupboards around the writing  surface, which is straight across the front with one long, or two or three shorter drawers in the frieze. The legs are long and tapered in accordance with late 18th century fashion.

Regency writing tables

Plain tables in mahogany or rosewood, with a little brass inlay and ornament, are more in our line of country than those mighty pieces decorated with the wildest flights of neo-classical fancy, turned out by fashionable craftsmen of the day. Some writing tables of the period stand on fantastic Egyptian-style figures—one at each corner—and the table top and frieze may be stiff with brass moulding in lumpy curls and swirls. Beautiful, perhaps, and certainly very grand; but not too easy to live with. Ordinary plain ones may be rather big and hefty as tables go—the top can be about four feet long and perhaps three feet wide—but they mix better with other pieces of furniture. These often have the central column support, standing on four short curved legs with castors, and there may be a drawer or two in the frieze. As desks they are not up to much, but they make good side-tables of the 'occasional' type.

Library writing tables

The 'drum' type of library table, with a round top, drawers around the frieze and sometimes bookrests, already has its place in Tables: 'Useful Large'; but there are several other types which are more at home in the desk section. The 'pedestal' style dates from the mid-18th century: this has a large rectangular or occasionally an oval top resting on two end pieces containing drawers and cupboards, with a space between rather like the kneehole. This space can have a recessed cupboard built into it which, like the kneehole desk gap, can be more trouble than it is worth: in the first place you cannot stretch your legs comfortably under the desk, and in the second place only a midget would consider the cupboard at a useful height. Still, you can't have too many cupboards. Early Georgian pedestal library tables can be lavishly gilded and extravagantly carved, but this didn't last long: later 18th century examples are much plainer, if just as large. Hepplewhite and Sheraton both liked round and kidney shaped tops, as well as the conventional oblong; and Sheraton also used the oval top. The two end pedestal pieces each have a cupboard and a shallow top drawer, and there may be another shallow drawer in the frieze above the knee space.

'Lady-like'

Lady's Screen Desk

This dainty little number was supposed to be a fire-screen as well as a writing desk: certainly the writer would be well-placed for burning incriminating letters; but on the other hand she would have no excuse for her guilty blush when confronted by her lord and master —one has a vision of the lady defending herself with her screen-desk as with a shield. It is a pretty piece, though, a small cabinet standing on slim standards joined by a narrow stretcher, each leg dividing to a bracket foot curving forwards and back. The cabinet may be about eighteen inches square and three or four inches deep, with a fall-front and a fitted interior of little drawers and cubby-holes. Many of the best examples are made of satinwood, but some are mahogany, and as the 18th century eased into the

19th, mahogany staged a come-back as the wood for such small, expensive items of furniture. They are still expensive, only more so; and that goes for the majority of 'lady-like' antiques.

Work Tables

Look under Tables: 'Useful Small', and you will find that some of these small sewing tables could do double duty as writing tables: they can have a fall-front as a writing surface, and the box-frame may be fitted up with little compartments for papers and pens as well as bobbins and needles. These were not as common as the sewing-bag sort shown in the picture, though.

Harlequin Pembroke table

If anything goes wrong with this particular table you may have to call in the engineers: it is a complicated piece of mechanism and rare and precious besides. Still, if you have one it can be a lot of fun and be worth a lot of money. On the surface it looks like a normal Pembroke table (See Tables: 'Decorative Medium') with slim tapered legs and hinged flaps supported by small wooden 'fly' brackets. The difference is this: if you look at the main top you will see that it is split in half across the width; then, if you reach under one flap and turn the fly bracket like a handle, half the top rises up and is seen to be fitted with little pigeon-holes and drawers; you then raise the flap and use it as a writing surface, ignoring the other half of the table altogether. When the fitted  super-structure is lowered again into the underframe the top of it becomes all one with the main top, and you can use the table for tea or anything else you like. Very natty.

Dwarf Cabinet

This is a narrow, spindly little desk on long tapered legs, made in satinwood or mahogany or perhaps hardwood, and very exquisite and fragile. The small writing top has a shallow drawer in the frieze; at the back is a low section of tiny drawers and pigeon-holes, with perhaps a small bookshelf over it. This item is strictly for the well-heeled dwarf: it is an expensive sort of status symbol.

Lady's Cabinet

This is a larger version of the dwarf cabinet, and more elaborately constructed. The fitted super-structure has a hinged front flap which lifts up and slides back into a narrow groove just above the top row of cubby-holes. The writing surface is double: the top layer swings over towards the front to rest on the drawer in the frieze which you pull slightly forward for the purpose. The bookshelf on top of the fitted section has a little set of drawers at each end, each set enclosed by a small door. This type was also made in satinwood or mahogany and, like all lady-like desks of the Sheraton era, beautifully designed and finished.

Lady's Cylinder Desk and Bookcase

This is the largest of the lady-like desks we call lady-like, but even this is not exactly practical or business-like. It is about two and a half feet across; the legs are slim and tapered, and the bottom of the table frieze curves in a very gentle arch—not a kneehole as such, but at least higher at the apex than at the sides. The writing surface and its back structure of drawers and pigeon-holes are covered by a cylinder front: this is a rounded cover on the same principle as the roll-top desk front, but made in one curved piece instead of slats backed by canvas. On the desk top stands a small bookcase with a couple of shelves, enclosed by two square glass doors supposed to be backed with draped silk curtains; and around the top of the bookcase runs a low brass rim.

Davenport

This style of desk was extremely popular in Victorian drawing rooms and there seem to be a large number going cheaply today. Unfortunately they are very uncomfortable for adult use, being only about two and a half feet high and two feet wide, but they make good children's desks if you can persuade them to use them. Davenports all look more or less like the one in the picture: the drawers run from side to side, not from front to back as on other lady-like styles; the sloping writing surface lifts up to show a shallow well for pens and papers, sometimes with a little drawer or two at the back; and there may be an extra side

drawer with a hidden spring lock. Apart from Sheraton-style copies, the Davenport was the only lady-like desk to emerge from the 19th century, and those you will see will be originals. It may take some time, but one day they will be highly priced antiques and as far from our reach as an original late-18th century desk is now. If you want a lady-like desk at all, a Davenport would be a thoughtful buy.

43

Chapter 5

Chests and Cupboards

CHESTS can either be the Dead-Man type, with the lid on which fifteen men sat, Yo Ho; or the type with drawers which stick infuriatingly and get pyjamas and things jammed down into the back space. Chests of drawers evolved from chests proper during the late 17th century: they are by far the most common type nowadays, and most of this section deals with the various styles and variations, but the old-style box chest is worth a mention first, even for those of us who keep pieces-of-eight in the bank.

Until it was displaced by the chest of drawers, the lidded box chest was used from very early days for storing linen, clothes, and household equipments of every kind. Before the advent of the trunk and the carpet bag we read of mediae-
val travellers loaded down with great wooden chests of belongings; and if Chaucer and Boccaccio are to be believed, chests came in very handy when husbands arrived home from the wars without fair warning. They come in all sizes, and on the whole they are bulky, heavy, and often decorated with rather clumsy, florid carving.

Box chest

Old chests are not very popular, but for the antique consumer, rather than the collector, they can be very useful indeed for storing blankets, rugs, children's toys and general paraphernalia—and they are very reasonably priced. A lady I know bought a monster chest to use as a window seat; it cost her less than having a window seat built in, holds mountains of stuff, stands up to endless kicking and bashing, and is genuine 16th century oak, no less. You might not be so lucky, but at least don't pass them by without taking a look.

Chests with domed lid tops, like Victorian leather trunks, are called 'coffers'; and coffers with two drawers at the bottom are called 'mule-chests', and it was from this hybrid formula that the chest of drawers as we know it finally evolved.

Chests of Drawers

(a) The earliest chests of drawers, dating from the *mid-17th century*, were nearly always of oak, and were often made in two sections, one above the other. The drawers in the lower stage were enclosed by doors, and the upper stage usually had one deep and one shallow drawer. The carved decoration on the door panels and drawers was geometrical in design, with mitred corners and squared-off projecting mouldings, and the piece usually stood on round bun-shaped feet. Very few of these early chests survive, and of course those that do exist are rare and precious indeed. Their most interesting feature is one which modern furniture designers would do well to copy: most of them have one very deep drawer for the express purpose of containing the large, plumed cavaliers' hats of the period; and while hats today may not be quite so large and grand, the problem of where to store them is one which crops up in nearly everybody's house.

(b) *Late 17th century* chests of drawers are much plainer than the early styles, with flat drawer fronts and little or no decoration. Oak or fruitwood examples were fairly common, especially in country districts, but many of the better chests were made of walnut or oak veneered with walnut, with plain brass drop or loop drawer handles. These late Stuart and William-and-Mary models were often placed on stands of varying heights, with twist-turned or bulbous-shaped legs and curved X-stretchers. The stand might contain one or more drawers; and a 'lowboy' stand would be a foot or so high, a 'tallboy' of table height. Fewer stands have survived than chests: the onslaughts of woodworm, which like walnut better than any other wood,

Early 18th century chest of drawers

combined with the considerable weight of the chests, saw to it that few stands lasted out the two hundred years between then and now. Chests without stands usually stood on low, bun-shaped feet.

(c) Chests of drawers of the *early 18th century* are similar to the William-and-Mary style, but those on stands had the cabriole leg of Queen Anne. In general the construction and finish is neater than the sometimes clumsy work of the 17th century, and walnut became ever more popular, though country oak went on for a good many years. Complex *marquetry* and *parquetry* designs were applied in various woods onto the drawer fronts of fine pieces. The dictum applied to other pieces of furniture applies here: don't expect an original; and it must be said too that none of these early chests seem to have been reproduced in quantity. It was left to Chippendale to supply the standard work which has been copied again and again by ardent disciples.

Chippendale chest of drawers

(d) Chests of drawers of the mid-18th century are among the most sought-after and expensive of their kind, but *Chippendale* styles have never been allowed to go out of fashion and you should be able to find a fair copy if you work at it. The wood is mahogany, the feet square, straight-edged brackets, and there

45

should be four long drawers or, more commonly, three long drawers and two shorter top ones. Serpentine-fronted examples are the most popular, but here you'll find yourself in expensive territory: stick to plain straight fronts and you'll still be able to pay the grocery bill. In theory the brass keyplates or '*escutcheons*' should be sunk flush with the drawer front, but if they are screwed on don't be upset—they look nearly as nice and if they drop off you can screw them back on again. Country-made originals of the period usually had wooden knob drawer handles, but you will probably find that these have been replaced by more typical brass loops— dealers don't like you to think that a piece isn't the real thing, and wooden knobs seem to be fixed in the public mind as Victorian. Such is antique snobbery.

(e) *Hepplewhite* chests of drawers are very plain and demure, with slender splayed feet curving out to merge smoothly with

Hepplewhite chest of drawers

the corners of the chest. Serpentine fronts are, as always, lamentably expensive, but you should be able to find a reasonable bow-front, and this may have a low, curved apron piece hanging from the bottom drawer frame between the two front legs. Small Hepplewhite chests are rare, and even small 19th century reproductions can be more expensive than big originals, so look for large sizes. The wood is usually mahogany, sometimes with slim bands of inlay around the drawer fronts, which may have small, circular brass handles.

(f) *Sheraton* chests of drawers follow the late 18th century vogue: his best-known style is the bow-front, usually made in mahogany but occasionally in satinwood or harewood. Fine period pieces are beautifully inlaid with lines of ebony and different woods, or elegantly painted with classical motifs; but plain Victorian or Edwardian reproductions would be nearer our hearts than the likes of these.

(g) Chests of drawers of the Regency period are usually in mahogany or rosewood (rosewood in the parlour, mahogany in the bedroom, was a bizarre dictate of Regency fashion). Unlike chairs and tables, the style in chests of drawers does not alter significantly from the previous one. Most are straight-fronted or bowfronted: the front may be framed by a pair of reeded classicalstyle columns; and there may be a deep frieze just above the two smaller top drawers, but these are minor indications of the Regency swing to classical-style furniture on a more massive scale than before. The curved bracket foot of the later 18th century gives way to a straight, rather high, turned foot; the drawer handles may be round rings fixed to lion masks, and the keyholes may have ivory diamond-shaped escutcheons around them.

(h) *Victorian* chests of drawers are rocks of the age—heavy, ponderous, and frequently big enough to hide a horse in. The top alone can be a couple of inches thick; the drawers solid mahogany, and the corner posts as thick as small tree-trunks. You could buy one of these for the price of the wood alone—and sharp dealers often do so, immediately dismantling them to make up other, smaller pieces of furniture sold as 'genuine' Chippendale or Hepplewhite to the unwary. All that is old wood is not old; but it is not difficult to detect a phony: the structure frame and the insides of drawers will look and smell suspiciously new if you take the thing to pieces and pry into it.

Batchelor Chests

This is the name given to that small chest of drawers—widely copied but still too expensive—which has a double top hinged in front and unfolding forward to rest on slides, like a bureau writing flap. The style dates from the early and mid-18th century, and the general effect is Chippendale. The price and popularity of these chests exceed their usefulness; but there you are. Just for the record, 'batchelor chest' can also mean one of those small tables with a hinged top lifting to show a prop-up mirror and a well for hiding one's wig in.

Brush Slide

Some tallboys have a sliding piece which pulls out just above the two top drawers of the bottom chest: this can be used as a writing surface or as a handy surface for brushing clothes on—have you noticed that if you lay clothes on the bed to brush them they pick up more dust? The brush slide is a clever notion, but unfortunately it has been extended to small reproduction chests which may be pretty, but pricey, and the slide isn't big enough to brush on effectively, believe me.

Military Chest

This is an early and mid-19th century piece; a four-square chest of drawers with brass handles sunk flush with the drawer fronts, and brass clips on the corners. There are no legs at all, and the whole thing is designed to stand up to the heavy wear and tear of travelling across the Seven Seas to build the Empire. Many are made in two sections, one resting on the other; and some have a small writing compartment in a central, drop-front top drawer. All very Kipling, and quite a burden, too, even for a White Man.

Tallboy

During the 18th century this was called a chest-on-chest, and that's exactly what it is. Early tallboys were in walnut; they reached their heyday in mahogany in the mid-18th century and were only gradually replaced in popularity by the wardrobe later on. The bottom chest of drawers usually has square, Chippendale-style bracket feet; the top stage stands as high again, and you wouldn't believe how useful the top drawers can be when you want to hide things away from prying visitors. A lot of people are cagey about buying tallboys because they look so enormous; but they take up no more floor space than a single chest of drawers, and you get twice the storage space for perhaps half the price of a singleton. Tallboys are relatively cheap—and many of those on the market are 18th century vintage, so they are good value for money. You don't have to dust the high top too often, either.

Wellington Chest

This is the name often tagged onto high, narrow 19th century chests with up to a dozen drawers. They are usually made of mahogany or rosewood, and an old one can be unexpectedly expensive, so don't get too carried away.

Commode

'Commode' is the ordinary French word for chest of drawers. It is used over here by a mercifully diminishing circle of enthusiasts who think that any French word is chic; but it is also the name given to chests of drawers in the style in which they were made in 18th century France. There is a steady vogue for these 'French-style' chests, so this is what they look like.

The three-drawer commode stands on short curvy legs; the two-drawer model on rather long, cabriole legs. The best known and most copied ornamental feature is *ormolu*, a furniture mount of bronze or brass, cast, chiselled and gilded, and then applied as decoration. Apart from lavish ormolu, French-style commodes can be decorated in the dizzy, frivolous mode called '*rococo*', with flowers and ribbons, shells, leaves and oriental motifs in fine marquetry work. They also have the '*bombé*' front, which differs from the serpentine front in that it curves from top to bottom as well as from side to side; and they may have marble tops. Up to now the French 18th century rococo style has been studiously ignored as such, but if you check back to pier tables, console tables and side tables in Chapter Three you will see its effect on English furniture fashion.

It is hard to tell the difference between the real thing and a good 19th century copy. Both are very expensive—just look at all that glittering ormolu and you will know why. But a bad copy can be very very bad. . . . If you still hanker for ormolu regardless of quality and cost, consider the idea that one lone piece in an otherwise plain room can look like a grin with one gold tooth.

'Commode' was used in England during the 18th century to describe chests of drawers with serpentine fronts, and also certain curvy cupboards in the French style. Chippendale produced a chest with carved corners which stood on a cabriole-legged stand

and Adam designed some very nice little numbers on short tapered legs, which have been copied by Edwardian cabinet makers of the early 20th century. This sort of parlour piece can be called 'commode' without embarrassment on this side of the Channel, but on the whole the fancy French pieces are better known as such.

Court Cupboard

The cupboard started life as a board for cups: old styles may or may not have doors, and the court cupboard, which was used from Elizabethan times to the beginning of the 18th century, varies accordingly. Some have two or three open tiers supported by four heavy uprights carved in the style of 16th and 17th century table legs; some have one or more of the tiers enclosed by doors. Although the open-tier style is often called a buffet, both sorts are court cupboards proper; and they are often made of oak.

Corner Cupboard

This is a triangular cupboard fitting into the angle where two walls meet. The front can be diagonal, or curved in a bow-front, with solid or glazed doors enclosing shelves for china, glass or silver display. During the first half of the 18th century small hanging examples of the corner cupboard were made in veneered walnut or *japanned* wood; later ones are usually mahogany, and they may be hanging or floor-standing. The larger models have solid doors to the lower stage, glazed ones above, and they make good drink cupboards for those of us who feel that all modern cocktail cabinets of the light-flashing, music-playing variety should be gathered up and hurled into the sea.

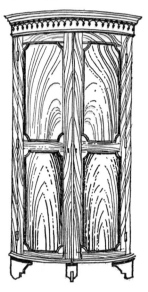

Display Cabinets

Display cabinets come in an infinite variety of shapes and sizes, but they all have glass doors, and shelves intended for showing off the family accumulation of china, glass and objets d'art. Such a cabinet may stand on top of a chest of drawers or on a bureau desk, but many stand alone as separate pieces of furniture, sometimes tall and narrow, sometimes much wider, with legs in various period styles. If the living room is lived in by children, it seems sense to place your display cabinet as far out of the line of fire as possible; and even then you can hardly be sure that your precious breakables will survive to see more peaceful days.

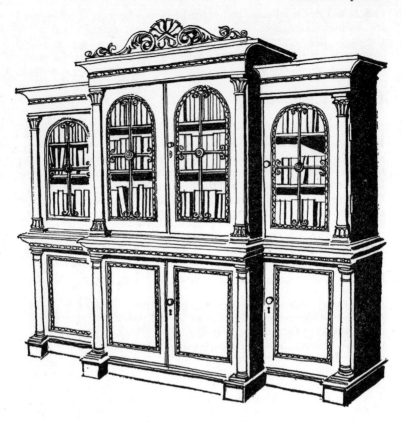

Breakfront Bookcase

This type of bookcase is made in three sections, the middle one projecting a few inches out from the two flanking cupboards—hence the 'broken' front line. They usually come in mahogany, with glazed doors in a tracery design and shelves for books behind them. Chippendale-style breakfronts can be eight or ten feet wide and alarmingly high and heavy: you'll need a lot of space, to say nothing of three men and a boy to do the shifting, but they certainly hold a lot of books. Later 18th century styles are lighter and understandably more in demand. Some models have cupboards below the bookshelves; others are entirely glass-fronted.

Regency Dwarf Cabinet

This is a low bookcase, either open or with metal grille doors, and often made and sold in pairs. They are usually mahogany or rosewood, sometimes with brass side handles or a little brass decoration. Originals are rather expensive, being small and neat as Regency furniture goes, but there seem to be a number of copies around in old wood which are not too ruinously priced.

Wardrobes

There is a lot to be said for having no wardrobe at all: built-in cupboards are preferable in every way but one: you can't take them with you when you go. Nevertheless, many people still want big hulking wardrobes, and old ones tend to be relatively inexpensive, so they merit a little study.

Clothes were laid flat during the Georgian era, not hung up on hangers as they are today; and the 'Clothes Press', as the wardrobe was called, was constructed accordingly. It had sliding shelves, or trays, in the upper section, and drawers below; but you will find that many such pieces have had the shelves removed and the drawers made false so that they will sell as hanging cupboards. Chippendale's 'gentleman's wardrobe' has shelves and drawers, short cabriole legs, and a plain top; the front is usually straight, but some curved fronts appear in the classier antique shops and auctions, and these are much more expensive.

Clothes presses were very common during the late 18th and early 19th century, but the wardrobe as we know it seems to have originated round about the Hepplewhite-Sheraton period of furniture design and it gradually ousted the press as the Regency merged into the long, long reign of Victoria. Both types are severely styled: Hepplewhite introduced oval door panels, which became even more popular at the hands of Sheraton; and door handles were usually engraved or embossed circles of brass. The wood is mahogany or mahogany veneer, and the feet may be short curved brackets like those on bureaux and secretaires of the day. Sheraton wardrobes proper may be 'break-front', like the bookcases mentioned earlier.

Victorian wardrobes tend to be much larger and clumsier than the earlier models. They may have three front panels, the middle one often filled with a large slab of looking-glass; the door knobs can be the size of cricket balls. Decoration varies according to succeeding Victorian fads: it goes without saying that the plainer the better. At the risk of sounding like a Handy Home Hint, it should be said that you could make, or have made, at least one good-sized dining table and a brace of coffee tables out of just one wardrobe: they are even more suitable for demolition and reconstruction than Victorian chests of drawers. The wood is good and the separate bits are big enough to put to good use elsewhere. If you feel inclined, that is.

Chiffonier

This is a muddling piece with endless possibilities: highly appropriate for winding up this chapter. It started out in late-18th century France as a ladies' clothes cupboard under the name 'chiffonnière'; and quickly evolved into a high, narrow chest of drawers. In 19th century England it was a small sideboard affair about three feet wide, with one drawer, one cupboard below the drawer and a back frame fitted with a shelf above. It may have a marble top; it may have a serpentine front; and the back may be a mirror in a carved frame. Chiffoniers like this are fairly common: you can use them as sideboards, bedside tables, or anything you like, and they are not too highly priced.

Chapter 6

'Country-Style'

UP to now all the talk has been of the Good Second-rate: furniture made in the style of the best but less so, in that it tends to be simpler, not such good quality and often made at a later date than the best pieces of a particular style. You may find that this class of antique furniture is called 'country' by some people; and the first-rate stuff is called 'town'; and you may also find, as I do, that such name-tags are both inaccurate and misleading. An enormous amount of second-rate furniture was made by minor craftsmen in town; on the other hand many first-rate pieces, if not actually made in the country, certainly migrated into the country to be used by country gentry. It is safer to label the distinction 'first-rate' and 'second-rate' and reserve the name 'country' for a style of furniture which is, exclusively, just that.

Country-style furniture is distinct and different from the mainstream of fashionable and would-be fashionable furniture. Made in the country for country folk, it is simple, serviceable and tough. Don't expect the classy woods like mahogany and satinwood: oak, elm, ash, yew and the fruitwood clan are more in the country line. After all, if you were a village carpenter in 1835 you wouldn't send to London for imported mahogany to make a dresser for Mr Archer the farmer: you'd use one of Mr Archer's oak trees or the rest of the elm you had left over from the parson's stable doors. Walnut was fairly common, but not in a stylish sense—in fact you will find few echoes of the world of fashion in this chapter. Carved decoration is kept to a minimum and there are no expensive extras like inlay or marquetry—country stuff is functional and definitely un-fancy.

Wooden stools, benches, settles and rough-hewn tables are so obviously country-style that there seems no point in running the full gamut of all their variations: you'll know them when you see them. But if you are thinking of buying a milking stool or an oaken settle or two you should start looking fast. There are sinister signs that the popularity—and the price—of old country furniture is rising. Country-style chairs are coming more and more into vogue as party pieces and conversation gimmicks for smart, stark interior design: the different types and the variation in pattern need to be sorted out before you rush to buy because you could be palmed off with a dreadful old chair the dealer found on the city dump. Then there is the business of the Welsh Dresser (lovingly reproduced year by year by the less imaginative furniture firms and faithfully displayed in exhibitions purporting to show the ultimate in contemporary furniture design) . . . oh yes, country style furniture is still going great guns.

Here is a pointer or two to be going on with.

Windsor Chairs

This type of chair is as tried and trusty as Windsor Castle, and over the last two hundred years it has changed about as much. It is a stick-back chair with a wooden saddle-shaped seat, simple turned legs set into holes in the seat bottom, and plain turned stretchers joining the legs for strength. The basic pattern appeared first in Buckinghamshire or thereabouts in the early 18th century and by the beginning of the 19th it had spread over most of the country. Back styles vary slightly, but that's about all, and you'll find a list of these over the page. The wood varies too: connoisseurs might consider a Windsor chair made entirely of yew wood to be a top-drawer model of its kind, but many different woods were used, often two or three different ones on a single chair. Thus the seat might be elm, the legs beech wood, the bent pieces fruitwood or birch; and I have a couple of Gothic-backed examples made in ash—as I discovered when I stripped off the neo-walnut stain and bleached the wood down to its proper colour.

The cabriole leg idea filtered through to the country craftsman in about the mid-18th century and from then on was used occasionally for the front legs, usually ending in pad feet but now and again the hoof foot of the 17th-early-18th century days. Stretchers, though, were not discarded as they were on more fashionable cabriole-legged chairs: these run from the front legs to the back and across the middle to form a horizontal H beneath the seat. Another type of stretcher bends inward from the two front legs to meet two short bars angling in from the back legs towards the centre: this is the '*cow's horn*' or '*crinoline*' stretcher.

Windsors come with arms and without them, and the sizes run from a big grandfather model to the armless 'kitchen chair' sort of thing you see all over the place. Although Windsor chairs abound in the second-rate antique trade—don't leave out the junk shops here, either—it seems very hard to get them in matching sets: two or three alike, perhaps, but seldom more. It may be sacrilege to some, but it is worth mentioning that they look remarkably smart painted or lacquered black or white or a clear bright colour. For the moment Windsor chairs are pretty cheap, often cheaper than Victorian dining chairs, but it would be tempting the gods of fashion to say how long this will last.

Here are a few back styles, but don't bother about them if you find them muddling: the basic fact to remember about the Windsor chair is the fact that the legs and back sticks are plugged into the seat—this is the Windsor hall-mark.

(a) *Comb-back* or *Fan-back:*
This is the earliest Windsor back pattern: a plain broad cresting rail fitted on top of the back sticks, of which there might be nine or ten. Up to the beginning of the 19th century the cresting rail was slightly shaped.

(b) *Hoop-back:*
Here there are two kinds of hoop to think about: the first and earliest, which appears on some comb-back Windsors, curves horizontally around the middle of the back and forward to form arm rests at elbow level; the second is the hoop-back proper, a vertical bent hoop forming the chair back outline and enclosing the back sticks. This type gradually displaced the comb-back in popularity, and the horizontal middle hoop was used with it for arm chairs throughout the 19th century.

(c) *Splats:*
Both the comb-back and the hoop-back Windsor chair can have a splat down the middle of the back, with three or four vertical sticks or spindles on each side. Early splats are unpierced fiddle or vase-shapes (narrower versions of the splats on fashionable Queen Anne and Early Georgian chairs, see Chapter Two); later ones may be pierced in simple designs (country cousins of the Chippendale-style splat seen in high society). The 'wheel splat' was the most popular: this is not a whole back filling but a tiny wheel pierced in the splat itself, which still has the clutch of sticks on each side. The Prince of Wales feather motif appears on some back splats too, but both this and the wheel design appeared many years after the fashionable styles which inspired them.

(d) *Gothic-back:*
This sort of Windsor chair-back dates from the mid-18th century and has been copied a lot since. It varies from a back filling of interlacing arches pierced à la Chippendale-Gothic, to a filling of three narrow splats pierced in the same manner, or even a pointed arch back outline in place of the usual hooped back. Whatever it is, it should call to mind those mediaeval cathedrals with soaring arches and high tracery windows.

(e) *Lath-back:*
This is basically a plain stick-back type of Windsor, except that the sticks are broad and flat.

(f) *Spindle-back:*
Strictly, the difference between a stick and a spindle is that where a stick is turned straight up and down, a spindle narrows in the middle and at each end, or else is fatter in the middle and slimmer at either end.

(g) *Elbow or Corner Windsor chair:*
This model is supposed to fit into a corner, and the back is only as high as the arm rests. The seat is diamond-shaped, with one leg at each side, one at the centre in front and the fourth at centre back. The low back curves round on three sides of the seat.

Ladder-back Chair

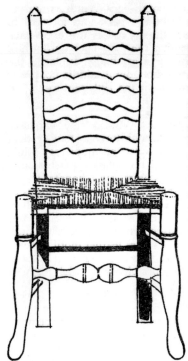

This type of country chair appeared during the late 17th century, when it was called a 'Dutch' chair; but the back idea as such is much older. The back slats run horizontally between the uprights like the rungs of a ladder: these slats may be plain and inclined to be rather rough but on better models they may be shaped into a wavy outline and sometimes even pierced in simple patterns. Early examples have low, heavy looking backs; later styles have the more typical high, narrow line. Common woods are oak, walnut, beech, ash and elm; and the seat is often cane or rushes woven over a wooden frame. The legs are sturdy and usually turned: the two back legs extend upwards to form the back uprights, and on armchair ladder-backs the front legs do the same to support the arm-rests at elbow level.

Spindle or Bobbin-back Chair

Another Homespun Hannah along the same general lines as the ladder-back, but here the back has two lots of five vertical spindles each, and armchair editions have three lots of five each. Spindles vary in shape and thickness from place to place about the country: on the whole they are gracefully turned and attractively shaped, and this sort of chair can be unexpectedly striking. The seat may be rush-bottomed, and the wood a home-grown variety.

Cricket Table

Three-legged cottage hearth stools were called crickets—and probably still are—and the 'cricket' table is simply an over-grown working version of the same. The pattern dates from the Middle Ages, and during the 18th century the same solid round top with simple splayed-out legs was fashioned in country workshops. Some have stretchers linking the legs, and a few have flaps extending in the same manner as those flaps on Gate-legs and Flap Dining tables in the classier models (see Tables), but in general the lily remain ungilded.

Dresser

Even if you and I don't prefix the word 'dresser' with the word 'Welsh', thousands do, automatically and with a vacant smile thrown in to set the seal of authority. So inextricably entwined have the two become that a cry to separate them is a cry in the wilderness: nevertheless the fact is that a dresser is a dresser is a dresser, and it may or may not carry details of decoration which may or may not be of Welsh origin. Any old country dresser will have local characteristics: this applies not only to Wales, both North and South, but also to different parts of England and indeed of France. So call it a dresser and call it a day.

The basic pattern has a high back with shelves for plates; a working counter-top and cupboards, drawers or both below. The wood might be oak, walnut, pine or various fruitwoods, and a piece might be decorated with a fretted frieze, carved panels, and some openwork piercing. Bearing in mind the possibility that none of the following features may appear on any dresser you see, here are some for the record:

(a) The *South Wales* dresser should have three drawers in the frieze below the dresser surface, and the rest of the lower stage should be open, with a 'pot-board' near the floor like the bottom tier of a court cupboard (see Cupboards). Spaced columns divide the open stage, and the dresser legs should be turned.

South Wales dresser

(b) The lower section of the *North Wales* dresser should be completely enclosed: it has two side cupboards and a tier of drawers down the middle. 18th century examples may have Gothic-arched door panels.

(c) The *West Wales* dresser should have two cupboards in the lower stage, with an open space between them.

(d) *Lancashire, Yorkshire and Shropshire* dressers may have small cupboards on the ends of the plate shelves—on the other hand they might not.

(e) Some models may have a row of spice drawers below the plate rack.

(f) Dressers made before 1800 did not normally have a solid back to the upper stage, but it may have been added to old examples, so look for plywood or matchwood additions.

(g) The drawer fronts of some dressers may be decorated with *cross-banding*, an applied border of contrasting wood; and an 18th or early 19th century dresser might have *cock-beading* on the edges of the drawers—this is a small moulding of half-circular section, applied to the drawer fronts.

A nice old 19th century dresser should be cheaper and a lot more interesting to have around the kitchen than slick modern units in formica and chrome, but it might look gimmicky and awkward anywhere else in the house. All the same, dressers are fashionable today in the interior decorating set—a pine one can cost a fortune as a 'quaint' piece on which to display ultra-modern glass and ancient knick-knacks. They can look very O.K. in the right setting, but be sure and buy an old one, not a ye olde copie.

Chapter 7

Whatnots and What Not

ONE or two of the following random selection of items can be adapted to an alternative use: a Canterbury music stand makes the best magazine rack yet devised, for instance; and a lead-lined wine cooler can always be filled with earth and a bay-tree if you feel inclined to cool your wine elsewhere. On the whole, though, most of the minor pieces listed here are specialised, in that they are designed to do one particular job and no other; and if the job is not available they are singularly in the way. You can't do much with a fire-screen if you rely exclusively on central heating to keep warm: it simply stands around waiting to be tripped over. The catch is that antique-hunters tend to think of such pieces as useful because they are comparatively small and look adaptable; in fact they are little more than conversation pieces fulfilling a decorative function only.

Again, people who would not dream of buying a set of Victorian dining chairs fall gleefully on a gilt-framed mirror or a butler's tray costing just as much, and carry it home in triumph. Fair enough, if you want a butler's tray and not a set of chairs; but remember that it is impossible to apply to pieces of this kind the no-nonsense consumer criteria we have applied to other furniture in this book. Small, sometimes eccentric antiques are popular status symbols: they perform, elegantly and therefore expensively, functions of a strictly unnecessary kind. If you have fourteen mugs with 'A Present from Scarborough' on them you will be sorely tempted to rush out and buy a whatnot to stand them on. On the other hand, you could stand them on the window-sill for free.

Whatnot

This is a 19th century piece: a small portable stand of three or four shelves supported by four corner posts, used for displaying ornaments, bric-a-brac and sometimes books. Whatnots come in mahogany or rosewood, and also in papier mâché or other novel materials of the Victorian era. The nicest ones are plain, but they can be lavishly—and hideously—decorated with carving, paint and gilt in Victorian flights of fancy.

Dumb-waiter

These date from the early 18th century and were very common in the 19th: the piece consists of three circular trays in sizes diminishing towards the top, supported one above the other by a central upright on a tripod base, like a Tripod table (see Tables: Useful Small) to the power of three. They were used as dining room stands and appeared also in Victorian parlours.

Butler's Tray

This is a tray, usually rectangular with a gallery fitted around the edge, on legs or on a folding stand. X-shaped stands were used from about 1750 on; and towards the end of the 18th century the tray top might be oval. Victorian models often have drop sides, thus forming an extra tea-table to add to the multitude of sofa tables, occasional tables and dumb-waiters considered essential in the 19th century household.

Canterbury

According to Sheraton, Canterbury music stands were so called 'because the Bishop of that See first gave orders for these pieces'. They were very popular in the early 19th century and are much sought-after today by antique enthusiasts who may or may not be tone-deaf. The Canterbury is a small stand on castors, or short legs with castors; it has vertical partitions for music books and song sheets and sometimes a small drawer below the divisions. Early  examples can be ludicrously expensive, but the style has been widely and usually successfully copied and good-looking reproductions are more fairly priced. They are very handy if you are an inveterate hoarder of journals and papers; but you could always clear a bookshelf or, alternatively put the stuff in the dustbin.

Dressing Glass

This is a small adjustable looking-glass designed to stand on a table or chest of drawers, the ancestor of the modern dressing table mirror, but a different type from those mirrors incorporated in an old kneehole dressing tables (see Tables: Useful Large). Styles vary slightly: the square-shaped model of the later 17th century gave way to an oblong glass with an arched top in a narrow frame, and from about 1700 it might be supported between two uprights mounted on a box stand. This stand may be straight or serpentine-fronted, perhaps with a couple of little drawers in it; but don't be surprised to find the type of dressing glass whose supporting uprights stand only on curving bracket feet—this sort continued to be made through the 18th and 19th centuries as well as the box stand examples. By 1750 mahogany was the usual wood; and after about 1760 satinwood came into fashion for such small items of furniture, though mahogany continued to be popular. Oval or shield-shaped mirrors on curved uprights were fashionable

during the later 18th century era of Hepplewhite and Sheraton; wide, oblong dressing glasses in mahogany or rosewood, swung between turned uprights, are characteristic of the early 19th century Regency period; and the Victorians copied everything available, besides producing a few florid styles of their own.

Cheval Glass

You can call this a Horse dressing glass if you want to—it comes to the same thing—but somehow Cheval sounds more glamorous. It is a full length, floor-standing looking glass swung between two uprights on bracket feet; the uprights are often linked by a stretcher just below the mirror frame and the mirror itself pivots on adjustable screws. The piece appeared in the late 18th century and was in great demand for Victorian bedrooms until someone hit on the notion of looking-glass panels in wardrobe doors: this simplified matters a lot, and the cheval glass suffered a decline. Most of them are good-looking and graceful, but they are too awkward to be very popular today in modern bedrooms. Still, if you feel unable to face up to any looking glass made later than 1900, even early examples of the cheval glass seem to be relatively inexpensive.

Wine Cooler

This piece was widely used from about the mid-18th century. It is a large wooden tub on four stubby legs or a solid base, lined with lead and used for chilling bottles of wine in water or ice. The shape can be oval, round, or square, sometimes brass-bound and usually with brass side handles. The popularity and price of wine coolers are both high, and matched pairs are at a premium, so try using the ice-box instead.

Firescreens

These came into use in the late 17th century, to protect delicate complexions from the fierce heat of large open fires. Nowadays they seem to be used primarily to fill up the fireplace when the fire is not burning: you'll see all sorts and conditions around, often sentimental relics of Great-Granny's handiwork.

The style, shape and ornament varies amazingly: the Pole Screen, an adjustable panel on an upright with a tripod base, was generally used in the 18th century; the screen can be oval, rectangular or shield-shaped, often beautifully painted or embroidered with family heraldry or prevailing stylish motifs. The Regency era of the early 19th century produced a model with the screen hung like a banner from a cross-bar on the upright: here the upright usually has a solid base. Yet another type is the Cheval Screen, resembling the Cheval glass (see above) in design, with two uprights enclosing the screen panel.

Victorian firescreens follow any and all these styles and the decoration is a monument to the industry of genteel 19th century young ladies who, since most things young ladies do nowadays were either forbidden or unheard of, spent their time ornamenting everything they could lay their hands on with beadwork, tapestry, embroidery, lacquering, painting, and seashells laboriously stuck on with glue.

Mirrors

Here are a few out of many different types and styles:

Queen Anne-style wall mirrors are fairly high and narrow: the frame is veneered in walnut and there may be a carved cresting piece over the top and an apron piece hanging below. Otherwise the decoration is restrained, apart from the odd shell motif.

The Early Georgian period saw the introduction of the convex mirror and the rise to grandeur of the pier glass. Pier glasses of the middle years of the 18th century could be seven feet high, framed in the extravagant rococo taste of the day with fantastic birds, scrolls, flowers, pagodas, even ruins and waterfalls, carved and gilded with a lavish disregard for discipline and hung over the equally fancy pier tables (see Tables: Decorative Medium) which stood between high, elegant Georgian windows. Adam pier glasses illustrate the classical vogue of the 1760's, with slender lines and delicate ornament; and this style continued to the end of the

18th century, when Regency became responsible for the heavier hand in decoration. When 19th century architects began to put bay-windows into houses pier glasses went out of fashion, but the Victorian habit of hanging a large mirror over a gilt-and-marble console table opposite the chimney glass amounted to almost the same thing.

Convex mirror

Round convex mirrors, topped by ferocious gilded eagles in carved wood or moulded plaster, were favourites in the 18th century and have been widely copied for the modern market, although the eagles are often conspicuous by their absence from the contemporary scene. The outer edge of the mirror frame should be reeded and gilded, the inner edge rimmed with black, and the moulding decorated with little gilt balls or perhaps a twisted-rope sort of ornament. Convex mirrors are not looking glasses in the normal sense: they should be hung so as to reflect a vase of flowers, a view into the garden or some pretty object which merits a mirror image in miniature.

Victorian mirrors range from huge gilt-framed chimney glasses in carved wood or papier mâché to quite small, neat numbers which could usefully be hung anywhere in the house. Towards the end of the 19th century the large, gilt-framed mantelpiece model was displaced by an ornamental structure of display shelves surrounding a smaller central mirror framed in wood; mirrors generally became less lavish, and looking-glass panels came into fashion for almost every kind of furniture, particularly sideboards, chiffoniers and display cabinets of the period.

Mirrors as a whole follow the decorative fashion of whatever period they coincide with: a vogue for chinoiserie, as occurred in the mid-18th century and again in the Victorian era, will produce a rash of pagodas and Chinese-style motifs on mirrors as well as furniture; and the same goes for Gothic, Classical and Rococo products of different periods.

Hat-and-Coat-Stand

Connoisseur antique buyers pass this by in bitter scorn; but there is no denying its usefulness in a house which does not run to a cloakroom, although its artistic merit may be seriously in doubt. The hat stand seems to have been unknown before the early 19th century and took some time to establish itself firmly beside the front door: its hour of glory coincides with that of Victoria and, with other Victorian eccentricities, it may be due to stage a comeback. The wood can be mahogany, rosewood or oak; the design and decoration vary astonishingly. One type consists of a heavy pillar with pegs at the top, a circular girdle around the middle which is pierced to hold sticks and umbrellas, and a tin drip-tray at the base. Another has wooden arms branching out from the pillar; and yet another incorporates a hall table with drawers for clothes brushes and a mirror above. Some examples resemble pagodas, some, twiggy trees; now and again a Gothic choir-screen looms out of the back of a junk shop with coat hooks extended in mute appeal. Such marvels are worth a look, even if you can't afford the house-room.

Wash-stand

Late Georgian and Victorian wash-stands, banished to attics and auctions with the advent of running H and C, are being resurrected for duties quite unconnected with their original purpose. Triangular corner wash-stands in mahogany, often with the old basin hole filled in, appear in modern living rooms as television tables and stands for flowers and books; and very smart and successful they are, too. Marble-topped rectangular wash-stands with cupboards below make excellent sideboards which cost a fraction of the price of Hepplewhite or Sheraton sideboard reproductions and, very often, much less than a slab of new marble—I paid thirty bob recently for a handsome Edwardian one in mahogany, marble top and all, and they are still one of the best buys available in the second-rate antique market. Apart from hefty, obviously Victorian-style examples, many 19th century wash-stands are elegant in the Sheraton tradition: slim tapered legs, uncluttered lines and no decoration beyond a little inlay (or fake inlay, which is painted onto the wood and can be indistinguishable from the real thing until you scratch it).

Compendium

A compendium, or 'lady's companion' can be a portable sewing box, writing box, cosmetic box, a box with chess or draughts or even, in very classy 18th century examples, a china tea service. In any event it is a box or small cabinet, often beautifully made and decorated and always fitted inside with a compact set of lady-like requirements for emergencies. Compendiums date from Tudor times, but pre-19th century examples can be wickedly expensive and even good-quality Victorian ones cost more than most people would willingly pay for a pretty box to keep things in. Medium-grade Victorian models, though, are more to the point here: they come in many styles, woods and types of fitting, and would make a good present for an untidy teenage niece, being models of compactness and neatness. Some have an upper tray with little wells for silver-topped glass bottles and jars, lifting out to reveal a deep well, like a small dressing case. Some have a folding writing surface over compartments for pens, inkstands and old love-letters; while sewing equipment can be incredibly complicated in variety and detail, with whole sets of scissors, bobbins, pincushions, a buttonhook, tatting shuttle and thimble. Dressing compendiums can have brushes for hair and clothes, scent bottle and powder boxes. There is often a mirror in the lid, and the interior may be lined with silk, satin or velvet. The box itself can be about 15 inches wide, a foot high and perhaps 9 or 10 inches deep, but the dimensions vary a lot and so does the material and decoration: some are leather, mounted on a wooden frame; some are veneered with different woods, and many are plain wood decorated

with brass, mother-of-pearl or tortoiseshell inlay. The more elaborate the compendium and the more complete its fittings, the more expensive it will be.

Compendiums and all the other bits and pieces covered in this chapter are essentially luxury items—nice, but unnecessary. They have nothing to do with furniture as known to the consumer; if you don't have them, you won't miss them. But because they seem to be minor items, costing relatively less than a major piece of furniture, the temptation to buy them is strong. Many an antique enthusiast has set forth to hunt for a desk which he badly needs and come home with a wine cooler which he doesn't need at all. This need not detract from his enjoyment of the wine cooler, but it does detract from his purse: he may see his dream desk the following day and have to pass it by because he cannot now afford it. Frittering money away is fun, but there are good and bad times for frittering; and the time to buy the items mentioned here is when you have your full complement of necessary furniture.

Chapter 8

Cool, Calm and Collected

No survey of antiques, however consumer-orientated, can possibly ignore the collecting bug. Antique enthusiasts tend to be particularly prone to this: you start out as a consumer in a quiet way, and the next thing you know you have thrown all your notions of usefulness and economy out of the window and replaced them with a burning desire to collect antiques for their own sake alone. I have nothing at all against this—collecting is very much more interesting and can afford amusement for a lifetime—but it is essential to realise that collecting antiques is a very different proposition from just buying a few to use.

To start with, the criteria are completely different. As a collector you couldn't care less about utility: your terms of reference are rarity, genuineness and historic interest. The items you buy to collect must show features characteristic of a particular period; they must be, if possible, 'good' examples of the work of that period in that the materials and craftsmanship are of the first quality. Best of all is the genuine piece of such rarity as to be unique: the collector may be prepared to forego top quality craftsmanship in favour of the rare and special. But if you collect Chippendale chairs you will not want to settle for a medium-grade example if you have a faint chance of finding a top-notch period piece, preferably one with a clearly-defined Chippendale eccentricity such as the Gothic back.

An important thing to grasp is that the expensive combination of good quality and rarity is not exclusive to the antique business. It costs a lot of money to produce a well-designed, well-made modern chair; hand-cut crystal vases cost more to make than those which can be turned out by the dozen from a single mould; good-quality materials of every kind do not come cheap, nor does the time expended in fashioning them. But there is only a limited number of people who can afford to pay the high prices asked for high-quality goods, with the result that there is, understandably, a limited supply of high-quality goods around. This was true in the beginning, is now, and probably ever shall be: it applies to the 18th century as well as the 20th, and to any other period in which the laws of demand and supply operated. We tend to forget that there is a very good reason, apart from the wear and tear of age, why there is so little good period furniture for sale today, and why it is so expensive: it is rare now, but it was rare also when it was new, because not many people could afford it then.

Besides the lure of age and rarity, collectors of antiques are motivated by other considerations which do not trouble the head of the consumer. You may collect because you happen to be passionately interested in 18th century brasswork and the social implications thereof; you may collect as an investment, in the hope that what you buy now you will sell later at a profit; you may simply collect for fun. Whatever your motive, it is a good idea to go out and carefully examine the possibilities open to you in the antique market as it stands today. Unless you are very rich indeed, the outlook is rather bleak in most of the obvious areas, and collecting without a plan of campaign is a sure way of winding up with a houseful of unrelated things you do not like.

A glance at the prices in any classy antique shop or at the Antique Fairs will be enough to tell you that you have missed the boat so far as well-known, 'fashionable' antiques are concerned. Furniture, china, silver, glassware and 'objects' of the 18th century, and earlier, fetch alarmingly large sums, very often regardless of quality and condition. Age alone puts up the price, and so does fashion: the last few years have seen a tremendous boom in the market as a whole and the dateable items sought by the collector are at a premium. All in all, the antique business has reached the proportions of a major industry.

For the embryo collector, deprived of the more orthodox forms of antique collecting by lack of funds, the Victorian and Edwardian eras offer happier hunting grounds. This period has not yet been officially recognised as 'antique', but it is nonetheless rapidly gaining status. If you want to collect seriously, whether as a possible investment or simply for the pleasure of having something which one day will be a rarity, you might study what is available from the 19th century, bearing in mind the rigorous criteria laid down by earlier collectors of earlier period productions. Besides the fringe benefits of the Victorian era—cardcases, picture postcards and the like—you might go for the mainstream items, such as furniture.

There is an enormous amount of Victorian and Edwardian furniture available, and a lot of it can actually be dated and identified to a particular firm of makers. The 19th century saw the beginning of fashionable furniture production on a much larger scale than ever before: the growing, wealthier middle-classes created a demand which was speedily supplied by enterprising manufacturers. If you are going to collect it, collect it scientifically, with lots of specialised books and catalogues and pages of glossy photographs. This way you will be able to sort out the various, complicated, distinctive styles: you should be able to pick out what is representative of a particular date. But the most important thing to look for is quality. Beside the Victorian craftsmen—and manufacturers could afford to be more lavish with his time and skill than they can be with his modern colleague—stood a modern-type machine churning out furniture for the lower end of the trade. It is no good buying a piece of Victorian furniture just because it is Victorian: what matters is that it should be a good-quality, identifiable, stylish example of its kind. This is a crucial factor in collecting 19th century pieces; the price is secondary, and you can't expect to pay bargain prices for excellent furniture of any date. For the moment, 19th century furniture remains on the periphery of the antique market, not smart enough to be fashionable and as yet not inflated in price. If you collect it, you should get the best pieces you can possibly afford, and they may turn out to be a shrewd investment after a while—though the operative word here is 'may': it may take five years, it may take fifty, it may not happen at all. You can't count on getting an investment bonus, but at least you can build up an intriguing collection to gloat over.

You can have a lot of fun collecting some of the 19th century fringe items, too; there are any amount of old lamps, samplers, fire-irons, wine labels and what-have-you on stalls and in countless shops devoted to the sale of bizarre and pretty oddments. Again, try to get the best examples you can afford: the best thing to do is to settle for one type of object—perhaps silver spoons or old Christmas cards—and collect the best ones you can find. There are countless Victorian bits and pieces which are amusing to collect, but don't expect them to be an investment or even of very much historical value for a long, long time. By all means collect glass bottle stoppers if you want to, but don't expect your family to scream with joy when they inherit five hundred and eighty-seven—and no bottles.

One last suggestion—what about collecting the contemporary? Even a Queen Anne chair was new once—though nobody ever thinks of it—and for all we know many people may have thought that Adam's designs were new-fangled nonsense, yet look what happened in a mere two hundred years. Modern design can be extremely good: there is beautiful glass, silver and china, as well as furniture, lovingly made by today's craftsmen to the highest standards. Most of us are still very sceptical of anything which does not conform to the accepted 'traditional' scheme of things, but this will not affect the antique hunter of the future, who will be scratching around looking for Barcelona chairs and getting as much pleasure out of stainless steel as we get out of 18th century inlay work.

If you don't want to collect anything, but simply want to buy a few antiques as a consumer, you make your own rules about what you want and why. The collector is bound by rules already laid down by others and he has no option but to follow them if he is to collect successfully. The common denominator is value for money: both the consumer and the collector are entitled to this, in antiques as in everything else, and from here on in it is up to you. So, like I said at the beginning—when in doubt, don't.

Glossary

Adam. Robert Adam (1728–92): eminent architect who designed furniture for the houses he built or re-modelled; famous for his revival of the classical style, based on Ancient Greek and Roman taste, begun in England during the 1760's.

Apron Piece. An ornamental piece of shaped and carved wood hanging from the seat rail of a chair or from the lower framework of a chest of drawers, etc.

Baluster Leg. A style of leg, shaped like a baluster, used on chairs and tables in the 17th century (see illustration).

Barley Sugar. An alternative name for **Twist-Turned** legs (see illustration) such as those on some late 17th century tables.

Twisted 'barley-sugar' leg

Bombé. A French term used to describe a swelling curve: the fronts of some later-18th century commodes and chests of drawers curve from top to bottom as well as from side to side; such fronts are called 'bombé'.

17th century baluster leg

Bracket Foot. A short foot attached to the underframe of a chest of drawers, bureau, tallboy, etc. The foot may be made in two pieces joined at the outside corner; the open side may be shaped, the corner side straight

Chippendale-style square 'bracket' foot

(see illustration) or curved in **Ogee** form. The term is also used to describe the short one-piece, curving foot seen on later 18th century furniture such as Hepplewhite chests of drawers and bureaux.

Cabriole leg with lion mask motif on the knee and paw foot

Cabriole. The name given to chair or table legs in the style of the first half of the 18th century (Queen Anne, Early Georgian, Chippendale): the leg curves out at the knee and inwards towards the foot, tapering towards the bottom. The foot may be a club, a claw-and-ball, a paw or scroll, and there may be a carved ornament on the knee such as the scallop shell or the lion motif (see illustration).

Cabochon or 'jewel and leaf' motif

Cabochon. A carved ornament used on furniture of the mid-18th century, especially on the knees of cabriole chair legs. The name comes from that given to rounded, uncut gem stones; the furniture ornament resembles one of these, usually oval-shaped and surrounded by scrolled, leafy carving (see illustration).

Capping. A square or pear-shaped piece at the top of some heavy 17th century chair and table legs.

Chinese Lattice Back. The name given to a particular Chippendale design for a chair back in the Chinese taste ('chinoiserie'). It was supposed to resemble Chinese fretted work and is an example of the highly romanticised vogue for Far Eastern styles and objects which swept fashionable circles in the mid-18th century (see illustration).

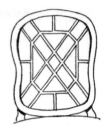

Chippendale-style Chinese lattice back

Chinoiserie. The term used to describe Western interpretations of Chinese styles in furniture, porcelain, textiles, etc. These were very popular during the 17th and 18th centuries up to about 1765, and again in the early 19th century to a briefer extent. Since then there has been a recurrence roughly every fifty years—the last was in the 1950's.

Chippendale. Thomas Chippendale (1718–79) designer and cabinet-maker; published 'The Gentleman and Cabinet-maker's Director' in 1754, reissued in 1755 and again between 1759 and 1762. He worked in London in St. Martin's Lane at the sign of 'The Chair' where his son (Thomas Chippendale the Younger) carried on the business after his death.

Claw-and-ball foot

Claw-and-Ball. This style of chair or table foot, a lion's or an eagle's claw clutching a ball, gained increasing popularity throughout the first half of the 18th century and has been used a lot since on reproduction pieces. It went out of favour for fashionable furniture with the classical revival of the later 18th century (see illustration).

Club Foot. A very plain pad foot used with the cabriole leg on many Queen Anne chairs and tables, and in general on much 18th century furniture where the cabriole leg appears.

Cornice. The projecting rim surrounding the top of a tallboy, bureau bookcase or any tall item of case furniture.

Cow's Horn. A type of stretcher much used on Windsor chairs: a piece of bentwood curves back from the two front legs to meet two short sticks angling forward from the back legs.

Cresting Rail. The top rail of a chair back.

Cup-and-Cover. A style of leg used in the 17th century (see illustration).

Cupid's Bow. The name often used to describe the curving outline of the cresting rail on Early Georgian and Chippendale chairs; an alternative to 'serpentine'.

Early Georgian. A term used here to describe the period of furniture-making between the reign of Queen Anne and the emergence of Chippendale as a dominant influence on style. It covers the reign of George I (1714–27) and most of the reign of George II (1727–60).

Escutcheon. Strictly, this is a shield with a coat-of-arms on it, but the word is often used for the key-plate surrounding the keyhole on a drawer or box.

17th century leg in cup-and-cover style

French Cabriole. This is a very light, slender version of the cabriole leg, much used on 18th century furniture in the rococo taste and later used on Victorian chairs.

Gadrooning

Gadrooning. A style of ornament used as a border decoration on furniture and on the rims of silver bowls, plates, candlesticks, etc. (see illustration).

Gothic Back. A particular Chippendale design for a chair back after the manner of mediaeval architecture, purporting to resemble soaring arches and stained-glass-window tracery. Used also on some Windsor chairs.

Hepplewhite. George Hepplewhite (died 1786); disciple of the Classical vogue inspired by Adam; designer and cabinet-maker. His 'Cabinet-maker and Upholsterer's Guide' was published in 1788, resulting in posthumous fame.

Chippendale-style Gothic chair back

Hipped. A style of cabriole leg on which the knee extends out as far as the edge of the seat rail of a chair or the frieze of a table.

Hoof Foot. A style of foot resembling a hoof, used on early cabriole-legged chairs during the reigns of William and Mary and Queen Anne. Such chairs were usually in walnut (see illustration).

Hoof foot

Inlay. A furniture ornament of bone, mother-of-pearl, different coloured woods, etc., set into the surface of a piece of furniture as decorative banding, patterns and designs. Much used on furniture of the later 18th century.

Japanning. A process of lacquering furniture in the Japanese manner, very popular in the late 17th and earlier 18th century. Bright colours and Eastern designs were used on English styles.

Chippendale-style ladder back

Jewel-and-Leaf. See **Cabochon.**

Ladder Back. A Chippendale chair back design of curved horizontal rails (see illustration). The name is also given to a style of country chair.

Lion Mask. A very popular motif for furniture decoration during the first half of the 18th century and again during the Regency period (see cabriole leg illustration).

Loop Handle. A curvy brass loop commonly used on mid 18th century drawers (see illustration).

Mid 18th century loop handle

Lyre Splat. A classical-style chair back filling in the shape of a stringed lyre (a lyre is the Ancient Greek version of a harp), used on chairs during the later 18th century and also as the leg support on some sofa tables and occasional tables (see illustration).

Lyre splat

Marquetry. This is *not* inlay, but a furniture veneer made of pieces of coloured woods fitted together into a design on the surface of a piece of furniture. Marquetry decoration was fashionable during the later 17th century, waned in the early 18th century, and waxed popular again between about 1775 and 1800.

Medallion. Small round or oval medallion motifs were popular furniture ornaments during the classical-style period of the later 18th century.

Ogee. A term used to describe an S-shaped double curve, particularly those on bracket feet as used on first-class mid-18th century case furniture (see illustration).

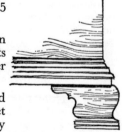

Bracket foot in ogee form

72

Ormolu. A word used for furniture mounts cast in bronze or brass and then gilded and applied as decoration. Ormolu mounts and objets d'art were the rage in French society of the 18th century, reaching a high water mark under the Imperial regime; and the ornament continued to be made and reproduced throughout the 19th century. English ormolu was never as fine as the best French products—but there is always a demand for 'French-style' furniture, and ormolu is practically synonymous with this.

Paw foot

Parquetry. A decorative veneer similar to **Marquetry,** but the patterns formed are *geometrical only*—marquetry designs may be flowers, birds, leaves and so on.

Paw Foot. This is another style of foot used with the cabriole leg on chairs and tables of the mid-18th century (see illustration).

Early 18th century pear-drop handle

Pear-Drop Handle. A small brass drop used on early chests of drawers of the late 17th and early 18th century (see illustration).

Pediment. An architectural term for the triangular end on a roof; also used to describe the decorative carved pieces on the cornices of bureau bookcases, tallboys, high cabinets etc. (see Adam-style illustrations).

Adam-style pediment with urn

Peg Top Foot. A style of foot often used on late-18th century chairs and on some Victorian chairs: the leg ends in a small rounded peg, often jutting out slightly from the main line of the leg (see illustration of French-style cabriole leg).

Quadrant. A metal pivot allowing a desk flap to move through a quarter of a circle only.

Queen Anne. A term used here to describe furniture styles of the early 18th century: Queen Anne reigned between 1702 and 1714; the styles continued until the 1720's.

Mid-18th century tapered leg reeded in the classical manner and ending in a spade foot

Reeding. A form of ornament resembling that used on classical columns; very popular for chair and table legs during the later 18th century. Reeding is the relief line on either side of a scooped-out channel—these channels are called 'fluting'; they run together in close parallels, divided by the 'reeding' (see illustration).

73

Late 18th century ring handle

Regency. A term used here to describe that period of furniture-making between about 1800 and 1840. In fact, the Regency began in 1811 and ended in 1820 with the death of George III; the Prince Regent succeeded him as George IV and was in turn succeeded by William IV in 1830.

Ring Handle. A brass circle commonly used on drawers of the later 18th century (see illustration).

Ribband Back. One of Chippendale's designs for a chair back, consisting of an intricately carved back splat of ribbon bows, knots and swirls (see illustration).

Chippendale-style ribband back

Rococo. A word used to describe an elaborate, fantastic style of decoration fashionable in 18th century France, and popular in England in the mid-18th century. Motifs included flowers, leaves, shells, scrolls and florid curves, such as those on the decorative friezes of console and pier tables, mirrors, etc.

Sabre Leg. The typical leg used on furniture of the Regency period resembling the curved sword called a 'sabre', or scimitar.

Scallop Shell. A very popular decorative motif for furniture, silver, etc. during the first half of the 18th century; often seen on the knees of cabriole legs of the period.

Scroll foot

Scroll Foot. A foot in the shape of a carved scroll, fashionable on mid-18th century chair legs (see illustration).

Sheraton. Thomas Sheraton (1751–1806), designer of light, delicate furniture fashionable in the late 18th century; published 'The Cabinet-maker's and Upholsterer's Drawing Book' between 1791 and 1794.

Shield Back. A later 18th century chair back in the form of a shield, enclosing a carved back splat; first used by Adam but usually associated with Hepplewhite chairs.

Spade Foot. A rectangular, tapered foot popular on late 18th century furniture legs (see reeded leg illustration).

Spindled. The name given to turned uprights and stretchers carved in curving lines: some spindle shapes are narrow at each end and broader in the middle; others are slim in the middle and broader at each end.

Splat. The central, vertical piece in a chair back; it may be solid, pierced and carved in simple designs or in a specific design such as the **Ribband Back,** the **Lyre Back,** etc.

Stretcher. The horizontal pieces connecting chair or table legs; some are plain, some shaped and carved.

74

Thimble Foot. A short tapering turned foot which vied for popularity with the SPADE FOOT—a rectangular version of the same idea—used on straight, slender late-18th century table and chair legs.

Three Ostrich Feather Motif. A decorative ornament patterned after the symbol of the Prince of Wales; used by Hepplewhite on many of his chair backs.

Tied Stretcher. An X-shaped stretcher form consisting of curvy stretcher rails running from table or chair legs to meet in the centre; a late 17th century feature.

Twist-Turn. A term used to describe an upright or leg turned in a spiral form, like a piece of barley-sugar (see **Barley-Sugar** illustration).

Wheel back splat as used on Windsor chairs

Urn. A motif much used as decoration during the classical revival of the later 18th century and particularly associated with Adam (see **Pediment** illustration).

Victorian. A term used here to describe furniture made during the greater part of the 19th century, roughly the period covered by the reign of Queen Victoria (1837–1901).

Wheat Ear. A motif carved in the form of an ear of wheat, often used on late-18th century shield-shaped chair backs.

Wheel Splat. A small wheel motif pierced in the back splats of many Windsor chairs (see illustration). Also the name given to a rare Hepplewhite chair back filling in the form of a wheel with spokes radiating out from the centre of the back.

Further Reading

English Furniture Styles from 1500 to 1830: *Ralph Fastnedge*
Old English Furniture: *Therle Hughes*
Old English Furniture: A simple Guide: *Hampden Gordon*
Small Antique Furniture: *Bernard and Therle Hughes*
Antiques for Amateurs: *C. G. L. DuCann*
Regency Furniture: *Clifford and Musgrave*
Victorian Furniture: *Symonds and Whineray*
Regency Antiques: *Brian Reade*
Victoriana: A Collector's Guide: *Violet Wood*
Georgian Furniture: *Ralph Edwards*
English Cottage Furniture: *F. Gordon Roe*
The Connoisseur's Handbook of Antique Collecting: *edited by Helena Hayward*
The Connoisseur Concise Encyclopaedia of Antiques: *edited by L. G. G. Ramsey*

Index

A

Adam, Robert and James, 13
Adam style: chairs, 15, 16
   tables, 24, 30, 31, 32, 33
Anne: see Queen Anne
Antique, definitions of, 8
Antique Dealers' Association, 9
Antique Fairs, 8, 9
Apron piece, 11, 46, 62
Armchairs, 21, 54
Arms of chairs, 17, 18, 19
Ash wood, 53, 54, 56

B

Bacchus, 19
Backs: see Chair Backs
Balloon-back chair, 20, 21
Baluster leg: see Legs
Barcelona chair, 68
Batchelor chest, 47
Beechwood, 54, 56
Birchwood, 54
Bookrests, 29
Bombé front, 48
Bookcase: see Breakfront
Bow-front, 26, 28, 46, 49, 51
Box chest: see Chest
Bracket foot: see Feet
Brass inlay, 19, 33, 35, 40, 51
Breakfast table, 31
Breakfront bookcase, 50
Brush slide, 47
Buffet: see Court Cupboard
Bureau:
   bookcase, 37, 39
   cabinet, 39
   desk, 36
Butler's tray, 60
Button-back chair, 21

C

Cabinets:
   display, 49, 63
   dwarf, 42, 50
Cabochon: see Jewel-and-Leaf
Cabriole leg: see Legs
Cane seat, 56
Canterbury, 59, 60
Capstan table: see Drum table
Card tables, 34
Carlton House writing table, 40
Castors, 25, 60
Cellaret, 33

Chair Backs:
   balloon, 20, 21
   bobbin, 55, 56
   buttoned, 20, 21
   Chinese lattice, 15
   comb, 54
   Gothic, 15, 55, 66
   heart-shape, 16
   hoop, 16, 55
   ladder, 15
   oval, 16, 21
   ribband, 15
   round, 16
   shield-shape, 16, 17
   spindle, 55, 56
   spoon, 21
   upholstered, 15, 16
Chair styles:
   late 17th century, 11, 12
   early 18th century, 12
   mid-18th century, 14, 15
   later 18th century, 15, 16, 17, 18
   early 19th century, 18, 19
   19th century, 20, 21, 22, 54
   Hybrid (mongrel), 18
Chest:
   batchelor, 47
   box, 44
   coffer, 44
   military, 47
   mule, 44
   Wellington, 48
Chests of drawers, 44-47
Chest-on-chest: see Tallboy
Cheval glass, 61
Chiffonier, 52, 53
Chinoiserie, 19, 63
Chippendale, Thomas, 13
Chippendale style:
   chairs, 10, 14, 15
   chests of drawers, 45, 48
   desks, 37, 48
   dressing tables, 28
   tables, 24, 29, 31, 33, 34
Clap tables: see Console
Classical style, 16, et seq.
Claw-and-ball foot; see Feet
Clothes press: see Wardrobe
Club foot: see Feet
Coffer: see Chest
Commode, 48
Compendium, 64
Concertina: see Card tables
Console table: see Tables
Convex mirror: see Mirrors
Cornice, 37
Country Chippendale, 15
Cresting rail, 12, 54
Cricket table: see Tables

K

Key plate, 46
Kneehole:
    desk, 38, 39
    desk and bookcase, 38, 39, 40
    dressing table, 27, 28
    writing table, 41
Knife case, 33

L

Ladder back: see Chair Backs
Lady's cabinet, 42
Lady's cylinder desk and bookcase, 43
Lady's screen desk, 41
Legs:
    Adam, 16
    baluster, 27
    bracket, 27
    bulbous, 45
    cabriole, 12, 15, 21, 24, 28, 32, 33,
        34, 45, 48, 51, 54
    'French-style' cabriole, 16
    gate, 27
    hipped cabriole, 13
    reeded, 17, 26, 33, 46
    sabre (scimitar), 19, 25, 27, 29, 35
    straight (square-section), 15, 16,
        17, 24, 31, 33, 34
    straight (turned), 16, 17, 26, 34
    twist-turned (barley-sugar), 24, 45
Library table, 29, 41
Lion mask motif, 12, 13, 19, 33, 46
Low-boy, 45
Lyre splat: see Splats
Lyre motif, 19

M

Magazine rack: see Canterbury
Mahogany, 13, et seq.
Marble top, 32, 33, 52, 63
Marquetry, 45, 48, 53
Military chest, 47
Mirrors: cheval glass, 61
    convex, 62, 63
    dressing glass, 60, 61
    pier glass, 32, 62
    Queen Anne, 62
    Victorian, 26, 52, 63
Mongrel chair: see Chair styles

N

Nests of tables, 30

O

Oak, 11, et seq.
Ogee: see Feet
Ormolu, 48

P

Pad foot: see Feet, club
Painted furniture, 17, 19, 34
Papier mâché, 29, 59, 63
Parquetry, 45
Paw foot: see Feet
Pediment, 37
Peg foot: see Feet
Pembroke table: see Tables
Pie-crust edging, 29
Pier glass: see Mirrors
Pier table: see Tables
Pillar-and-claw support, 25, 31, 35
Pine, 37, 57, 58
Plate warmer, 33
Prince of Wales motif, 16, 17, 55

Q

Quadrant, 40
Quartetto: see Nests of tables
Queen Anne:
    bureaux, 36, 37
    chairs, 12
    chests of drawers, 45
    mirrors, 62
    tables, 43

R

Reeding, 17, 26, 33, 46
Regency style:
    chairs, 18
    chests of drawers, 46
    dressing tables, 28
    tables, 25, 27, 30, 31, 32, 33, 35
    work tables, 31
    writing tables, 40
Reproductions, 8, 19, 20, 22, 25, 29
Ribband back: see Chair Backs
Rococo, 48, 62, 63
Rosewood, 17, et seq.

S

Sabre leg: see Legs
Satinwood, 16, et seq.
Satyr mask motif, 13
Scallop shell motif, 12
Scimitar leg: see Legs, sabre
Scott, Sir Walter, 19
Screen desk, 41
Scroll foot: see Feet
Scrolled arm, 19
Seats:
    cane, 56
    drop-in, 12, 20
    upholstered, 12, 20
    wooden, 15, 54